DATE DUE

GAYLORD			PRINTED IN U S A

ASPECTS OF LITERATURE

ASPECTS OF
LITERATURE

BY

JOHN MIDDLETON MURRY

Essay Index Reprint Series

BOOKS FOR LIBRARIES PRESS
FREEPORT, NEW YORK

First Published 1920
Reprinted 1970

INTERNATIONAL STANDARD BOOK NUMBER:
0-8369-1838-X

LIBRARY OF CONGRESS CATALOG CARD NUMBER:
79-128280

PRINTED IN THE UNITED STATES OF AMERICA

TO
BRUCE RICHMOND
TO WHOSE GENEROUS ENCOURAGEMENT
I OWE SO MUCH

Preface

Two of these essays, 'The Function of Criticism' and 'The Religion of Rousseau,' were contributed to the *Times Literary Supplement*; that on 'The Poetry of Edward Thomas' in the *Nation*; all the rest save one have appeared in the *Athenæum*.

The essays are arranged in the order in which they were written, with two exceptions. The second part of the essay on Tchehov has been placed with the first for convenience, although in order of thought it should follow the essay, 'The Cry in the Wilderness.' More important, I have placed 'The Function of Criticism' first although it was written last, because it treats of the broad problem of literary criticism, suggests a standard of values implicit elsewhere in the book, and thus to some degree affords an introduction to the remaining essays.

But the degree is not great, as the critical reader will quickly discover for himself. I ask him not to indulge the temptation of convicting me out of my own mouth. I am aware that my practice is often inconsistent with my professions; and I ask the reader to remember that the professions were made after the practice and to a considerable extent as the result of it. The practice came first, and if I could reasonably expect so much of the reader I would ask him to read 'The Function of Criticism' once more when he has reached the end of the book.

I make no apology for not having rewritten the essays. As a critic I enjoy nothing more than to trace

Preface

the development of a writer's attitude through its various phases; I could do no less than afford my readers the opportunity of a similar enjoyment in my own case. They may be assured that none of the essays have suffered any substantial alteration, even where, for instance in the case of the incidental and (I am now persuaded) quite inadequate estimate of Chaucer in 'The Nostalgia of Mr Masefield,' my view has since completely changed. Here and there I have recast expressions which, though not sufficiently conveying my meaning, had been passed in the haste of journalistic production. But I have nowhere tried to adjust earlier to later points of view.

I am aware that these points of view are often difficult to reconcile; that, for instance, ' æsthetic ' in the essay on Tchehov has a much narrower meaning than it bears in 'The Function of Criticism '; that the essay on ' The Religion of Rousseau ' is criticism of a kind which I deprecate as insufficient in the essay, ' The Cry in the Wilderness,' because it lacks that reference to life as a whole which I have come to regard as essential to criticism; and that in this latter essay I use the word ' moral ' (for instance in the phrase ' The values of literature are in the last resort moral ') in a sense which is never exactly defined. The key to most of these discrepancies will, I hope, be found in the introductory essay on ' The Function of Criticism.'

May, 1920.

Contents

ix

The Function of Criticism

It is curious and interesting to find our younger men of letters actively concerned with the present condition of literary criticism. This is a novel preoccupation for them and one which is, we believe, symptomatic of a general hesitancy and expectation. In the world of letters everything is a little up in the air, volatile and uncrystallised. It is a world of rejections and velleities; in spite of outward similarities, a strangely different world from that of half a dozen years ago. Then one had a tolerable certainty that the new star, if the new star was to appear, would burst upon our vision in the shape of a novel. To-day we feel it might be anything. The cloud no bigger than a man's hand might even be, like Trigorin's in ' The Sea-gull,' like a piano ; it has no predetermined form.

This sense of incalculability, which has been aroused by the prodigious literary efflorescence of late years, reacts upon its cause; and the reaction tends by many different paths to express itself finally in the ventilation of problems that hinge about criticism. There is a general feeling that the growth of the young plant has been too luxuriant; a desire to have it vigorously pruned by a capable gardener, in order that its strength may be gathered together to produce a more perfect fruit. There is also a sense that if the *lusus naturæ*, the writer of genius, were to appear, there ought to be a person or an organisation capable of recognising him, however unexpected his scent or the shape of his leaves. Both these tasks fall upon

I

criticism. The younger generation looks round a little apprehensively to see if there is a gardener whom it can trust, and decides, perhaps a little prematurely, that there is none.

There is reviewing, but no criticism, says one icy voice that we have learned to respect. There are pontiffs and potential pontiffs, but no critics, says another disrespectful young man. Oh, for some more Scotch Reviewers to settle the hash of our English bards, sighs a third. And the *London Mercury*, after whetting our appetite by announcing that it proposed to restore the standards of authoritative criticism, still leaves us a little in the dark as to what these standards are. Mr T. S. Eliot deals more kindly, if more frigidly, with us in the *Monthly Chapbook*. There are, he says, three kinds of criticism—the historical, the philosophic, and the purely literary.

'Every form of genuine criticism is directed towards creation. The historical or philosophic critic of poetry is criticising poetry in order to create a history or a philosophy; the poetic critic is criticising poetry in order to create poetry.'

These separate and distinct kinds, he considers, are but rarely found to-day, even in a fragmentary form; where they do exist, they are almost invariably mingled in an inextricable confusion.

Whether we agree or not with the general condemnation of reviewing implicit in this survey of the situation, or with the division of criticism itself, we have every reason to be grateful to Mr Eliot for disentangling the problem for us. The question of

2

criticism has become rather like Glaucus the sea-god, encrusted with shells and hung with weed till his lineaments are hardly discernible. We have at least a clear sight of him now, and we are able to decide whether we will accept Mr Eliot's description of him. Let us see.

We have no difficulty in agreeing that historical criticism of literature is a kind apart. The historical critic approaches literature as the manifestation of an evolutionary process in which all the phases are of equal value. Essentially, he has no concern with the greater or less literary excellence of the objects whose history he traces—their existence is alone sufficient for him; a bad book is as important as a good one, and much more important than a good one if it exercised, as bad books have a way of doing, a real influence on the course of literature. In practice, it is true, the historical critic generally fails of this ideal of unimpassioned objectivity. He either begins by making judgments of value for himself, or accepts those judgments which have been endorsed by tradition. He fastens upon a number of outstanding figures and more or less deliberately represents the process as from culmination to culmination; but in spite of this arbitrary foreshortening he is primarily concerned, in each one of the phases which he distinguishes, with that which is common to every member of the group of writers which it includes. The individuality, the quintessence, of a writer lies completely outside his view.

We may accept the isolation of the historical critic then, at least in theory, and conceive of him as a fragment of a social historian, as the author of a chapter in the history of the human spirit. But can we isolate the philosophic critic in the same way? And what exactly *is* a philosophic critic? Is he a critic with a philosophical scheme in which art and literature have their places, a critic who therefore approaches literature with a definite conception of it as one among many parallel manifestations of the human spirit, and with a system of values derived from his metaphysical scheme? Hegel and Croce are philosophical critics in this sense, and Aristotle is not, as far as we can judge from the Poetics, wherein he considers the literary work of Greece as an isolated phenomenon, and examines it in and for itself. But for the moment, and with the uneasy sense that we have not thoroughly laid the ghost of philosophic criticism, we will assume that we have isolated him, and pass to the consideration of the pure literary critic, if indeed we can find him.

What does he do? How shall we recognise him? Mr Eliot puts before us Coleridge and Aristotle and Dryden as literary critics *par excellence* arranged in an ascending scale of purity. The concatenation is curious, for these were men possessed of very different interests and faculties of mind; and it would occur to few to place Dryden, as a critic, at their head. The living centre of Aristotle's criticism is a conception of art as a means to a good life. As an activity, poetry ' is more philosophic than history,' a nearer approach to the universal truth in appearances; and as a more active influence, drama refines our spiritual being by a purgation of pity and terror. Indeed, it would not be an exaggeration to say that the very pith and marrow of Aristotle's literary criticism is a system of

4

moral values derived from his contemplation of life. It was necessary that this relation should exist, because for Aristotle literature was, essentially, an imitation of life, though we must remember to understand imitation according to our final sense of the theme which is the golden, persistent thread throughout the Poetics. The imitation of life in literature was for Aristotle, the creative revelation of the ideal actively at work in human life. The tragic hero failed because his composition was less than ideal; but he could only be a tragic hero if the ideal was implicit in him and he visibly approximated to it. It is this constant reference to the ideal which makes of 'imitation' a truly creative principle and the one which, properly understood, is the most permanently valid and pregnant of all; it is also one which has been constantly misunderstood. Its importance is, nevertheless, so central that adequate recognition of it might conceivably be taken as the distinguishing mark of all fruitful criticism.

To his sympathetic understanding of this principle Coleridge owed a great debt. It is true that his efforts to refine upon it were not only unsuccessful, but a trifle ludicrous; his effort to graft the vague transcendentalism of Germany on to the rigour and clarity of Aristotle was, from the outset, unfortunately conceived. But the root of the matter was there, and in Coleridge's fertile mind the Aristotelian theory of imitation flowered into a magnificent conception of the validity and process of the poetic imagination. And partly because the foundation was truly Aristotelian, partly because Coleridge had known what it was to be a great poet, the reference to life pervades

5

the whole of what is permanently valuable in Coleridge's criticism. In him, too, there is a strict and mutually fertilising relation between the moral and the æsthetic values. This is the firm ground beneath his feet when he—too seldom—proceeds to the free exercise of his exquisite æsthetic discrimination.

In Dryden, however, there was no such organic interpenetration. Dryden, too, had a fine sensibility, though less exquisite, by far, than that of Coleridge; but his theoretical system was not merely alien to him—it was in itself false and mistaken. *Corruptio optimi pessima.* He took over from France the sterilised and lifeless Aristotelianism which has been the plague of criticism for centuries; he used it no worse than his French exemplars, but he used it very little better than they. It was in his hands, as in theirs, a dead mechanical framework of rules about the unities. Dryden, we can see in his critical writing, was constantly chafed by it. He behaves like a fine horse with a bearing rein: he is continually tossing his head after a minute or two of ' good manners and action,' and saying, ' Shakespeare was the best of them, anyhow '; ' Chaucer beats Ovid to a standstill.' It is a gesture with which all decent people sympathise, and when it is made in language so supple as Dryden's prose it has a lasting charm. Dryden's heart was in the right place, and he was not afraid of showing it; but that does not make him a critic, much less a critic to be set as a superior in the company of Aristotle and Coleridge.

Our search for the pure literary critic is likely to be arduous. We have seen that there is a sense in which Dryden is a purer literary critic than either

6

Coleridge or Aristotle; but we have also seen that it is precisely by reason of the ' pureness ' in him that he is to be relegated into a rank inferior to theirs. It looks as though we might have to pronounce that the true literary critic is the philosophic critic. Yet the pronouncement must not be prematurely made; for there is a real and vital difference between those for whom we have accepted the designation of philosophic critics, Hegel or Croce, and Aristotle or Coleridge. Yet three of these (and it might be wise to include Coleridge as a fourth) were professional philosophers. It is evidently not the philosophy as such that makes the difference.

The difference depends, we believe, upon the nature of the philosophy. The secret lies in Aristotle. The true literary critic must have a humanistic philosophy. His inquiries must be modulated, subject to an intimate, organic governance, by an ideal of the good life. He is not the mere investigator of facts; existence is never for him synonymous with value, and it is of the utmost importance that he should never be deluded into believing that it is. He will not accept from Hegel the thesis that all the events of human history, all man's spiritual activities, are equally authentic manifestations of Spirit; he will not even recognise the existence of Spirit. He may accept from Croce the thesis that art is the expression of intuitions, but he will not be extravagantly grateful, because his duty as a critic is to distinguish between intuitions and to decide that one is more significant than another. A philosophy of art that lends him no aid in this and affords no indication why the expression of one intuition should be preferred to the expression of another is of little value to him. He will incline to say that Hegel and Croce are the scientists of art rather than its philosophers.

Here, then, is the opposition: between the philosophy that borrows its values from science and the philosophy which shares its values with art. We may put it with more cogency and truth : the opposition lies between a philosophy without values and a philosophy based upon them. For values are human, anthropocentric. Shut them out once and you shut them out for ever. You do not get them back, as some believe, by declaring that such and such a thing is true. Nothing is precious because it is true save to a mind which has, consciously or unconsciously, decided that it is good to know the truth. And the making of that single decision is a most momentous judgment of value. If the scientist appeals to it, as indeed he invariably does, he too is at bottom, though he may deny it, a humanist. He would do better to confess it, and to confess that he too is in search of the good life. Then he might become aware that to search for the good life is in fact impossible, unless he has an ideal of it before his mind's eye.

An ideal of the good life, if it is to have the internal coherence and the organic force of a true ideal, *must inevitably be æsthetic.* There is no other power than our æsthetic intuition by which we can imagine or conceive it; we can express it only in æsthetic terms. We say, for instance, the good life is that in which man has achieved a harmony of the diverse elements in his soul. For the good life, we know instinctively, is one of our human absolutes. It is not good with reference to any end outside itself.

8

The Function of Criticism

A man does not live the good life because he is a good citizen; but he is a good citizen because he lives the good life. And here we touch the secret of the most magnificently human of all books that has ever been written—Plato's *Republic*. In the *Republic* the good life and the life of the good citizen are identified; but the citizenship is not of an earthly but of an ideal city, whose proportions, like the duties of its citizens, are determined by the æsthetic intuition. Plato's philosophy is æsthetic through and through, and because it is æsthetic it is the most human, the most permanently pregnant of all philosophies. Much labour has been spent on the examination of the identity which Plato established between the good and the beautiful. It is labour lost, for that identity is axiomatic, absolute, irreducible. The Greeks knew by instinct that it is so, and in their common speech the word for a gentleman was the καλὸς κἀγαθός, the beautiful-good.

This is why we have to go back to the Greeks for the principles of art and criticism, and why only those critics who have returned to bathe themselves in the life-giving source have made enduring contributions to criticism. They alone are—let us not say philosophic critics but—critics indeed. Their approach to life and their approach to art are the same; to them, and to them alone, life and art are one. The interpenetration is complete; the standards by which life and art are judged the same. If we may use a metaphor, in the Greek view art is the consciousness of life. Poetry is more philosophic and more highly serious than history, just as the mind of a man is more significant than his outward gestures. To make those gestures significant the art of the actor must be called into play. So to make the outward event of history significant the poet's art is needed. Therefore a criticism which is based on the Greek view is impelled to assign to art a place, the place of sovereignty in its scheme of values. That Plato himself did not do this was due to his having misunderstood the nature of that process of ' imitation ' in which art consists; but only the superficial readers of Plato —and a good many readers deserve no better name —will conclude from the fact that he rejected art that his attitude was not fundamentally æsthetic. Not only is the *Republic* itself one of the greatest ' imitations,' one of the most subtle and profound works of art ever created, but it would also be true to say that Plato cleared the way for a true conception of art. In reality he rejected not art, but false art; and it only remained for Aristotle to discern the nature of the relation between artistic ' imitation ' and the ideal for the Platonic system to be complete and four-square, a perpetual inspiration and an everlasting foundation for art and the criticism of art.

Art, then, is the revelation of the ideal in human life. As the ideal is active and organic so must art itself be. The ideal is never achieved, therefore the process of revealing it is creative in the truest sense of the word. More than that, only by virtue of the artist in him can man appreciate or imagine the ideal at all. To discern it is essentially the work of divination or intuition. The artist divines the end at which human life is aiming; he makes men who are his characters completely expressive of themselves, which no actual man ever has been. If he works on a smaller canvas he aims to make himself completely expressive of himself. That, also, is the aim of the greater artist who expresses himself through the medium of a world of characters of his own creation. He needs that machinery, if a coarse and non-organic metaphor may be tolerated, for the explication of his own intuitions of the ideal, which are so various that the attempt to express them through the *persona* of himself would inevitably end in confusion. That is why the great poetic genius is never purely lyrical, and why the greatest lyrics are as often as not the work of poets who are only seldom lyrical.

Moreover, every act of intuition or divination of the ideal in act in the world of men must be set, implicitly or explicitly, in relation to the absolute ideal. In subordinating its particular intuitions to the absolute ideal art is, therefore, merely asserting its own sovereign autonomy. True criticism is itself an organic part of the whole activity of art; it is the exercise of sovereignty by art upon itself, and not the imposition of an alien. To use our previous metaphor, as art is the consciousness of life, criticism is the consciousness of art. The essential activity of true criticism is the harmonious control of art by art. This is at the root of a confusion in the thought of Mr Eliot, who, in his just anxiety to assert the full autonomy of art, pronounces that the true critic of poetry is the poet and has to smuggle the anomalous Aristotle in on the hardly convincing ground that 'he wrote well about everything,' and has, moreover, to elevate Dryden to a purple which he is quite unfitted to wear. No, what distinguishes the true critic of poetry is a truly æsthetic philosophy. In the

11

present state of society it is extremely probable that only the poet or the artist will possess this, for art and poetry were never more profoundly divorced from the ordinary life of society than they are at the present day. But the poet who would be a critic has to make his æsthetic philosophy conscious to himself; to him as a poet it may be unconscious. This necessary change from unconsciousness to consciousness is by no means easy, and we should do well to insist upon its difficulty, for quite as much nonsense is talked about poetry by poets and by artists about art as by the profane about either. Moreover, it is important to remember that in proportion as society approaches the ideal—there is no continual progress towards the ideal; at present society is as far removed from it as it has ever been—the chance of the philosopher, of the scientist even, becoming a true critic of art grows greater. When the æsthetic basis of all humane activity is familiarly recognised, the values of the philosopher, the scientist, and the artist become consciously the same, and therefore interchangeable.

Still, the ideal society is sufficiently remote for us to disregard it, and we shall say that the principle of art for art's sake contains an element of truth when it is opposed to those who would inflict upon art the values of science, of metaphysics, or of a morality of mere convention. We shall also say that the principle of art for art's sake needs to be understood and interpreted very differently. Its implications are tremendous. Art is autonomous, and to be pursued for its own sake, precisely because it comprehends the whole of human life; because it has reference to a more perfectly human morality than any other activity of man; because, in so far as it is truly art, it is indicative of a more comprehensive and unchallengeable harmony in the spirit of man. It does not demand impossibilities, that man should be at one with the universe or in tune with the infinite; but it does envisage the highest of all attainable ideals, that man should be at one with himself, obedient to his own most musical law.

Thus art reveals to us the principle of its own governance. The function of criticism is to apply it. Obviously it can be applied only by him who has achieved, if not the actual æsthetic ideal in life, at least a vision and a sense of it. He alone will know that the principle he has to elucidate and apply is living, organic. It is indeed the very principle of artistic creation itself. Therefore he will approach what claims to be a work of art first as a thing in itself, and seek with it the most intimate and immediate contact in order that he may decide whether it too is organic and living. He will be untiring in his effort to refine his power of discrimination by the frequentation of the finest work of the past, so that he may be sure of himself when he decides, as he must, whether the object before him is the expression of an æsthetic intuition at all. At the best he is likely to find that it is mixed and various; that fragments of æsthetic vision jostle with unsubordinated intellectual judgments.

But, in regarding the work of art as a thing in itself, he will never forget the hierarchy of comprehension, that the active ideal of art is indeed to see life steadily and see it whole, and that only he has a claim to the title of a great artist whose work manifests an incessant growth from a merely personal immediacy to a coherent and all-comprehending attitude to life. The great artist's work is in all its parts a revelation of the ideal as a principle of activity in human life. As the apprehension of the ideal is more or less perfect, the artist's comprehension will be greater or less. The critic has not merely the right, but the duty, to judge between Homer and Shakespeare, between Dante and Milton, between Cezanne and Michelangelo, Beethoven and Mozart. If the foundations of his criticism are truly æsthetic, he is compelled to believe and to show that among would-be artists some are true artists and some are not, and that among true artists some are greater than others. That what has generally passed under the name of æsthetic criticism assumes as an axiom that every true work of art is unique and incomparable is merely the paradox which betrays the unworthiness of such criticism to bear the name it has arrogated to itself. The function of true criticism is to establish a definite hierarchy among the great artists of the past, as well as to test the production of the present; by the combination of these activities it asserts the organic unity of all art. It cannot honestly be said that our present criticism is adequate to either task. [APRIL, 1920.

The Religion of Rousseau

THESE are times when men have need of the great solitaries; for each man now in his moment is a prey to the conviction that the world and his deepest aspirations are incommensurable. He is shaken by a presentiment that the lovely bodies of men are being spent and flaming human minds put out in a conflict for something which never can be won in the clash of material arms, and he is distraught by a vision of humanity as a child pitifully wandering in a dark wood where the wind faintly echoes the strange word ' Peace.' Therefore he too wanders pitifully like that child, seeking peace, and men are become the symbols of mankind. The tragic paradox of human life which slumbers in the soul in years of peace is awakened again. When we would be solitary and cannot, we are made sensible of the depth and validity of the impulse which moved the solitaries of the past.

The paradox is apparent now on every hand. It appears in the death of the author of *La Formation Réligieuse de J.-J. Rousseau.*[1] One of the most distinguished of the younger generation of French scholar-critics, M. Masson met a soldier's death before the book to which he had devoted ten years of his life was published. He had prepared it for the press in the leisure hours of the trenches. There he had communed with the unquiet spirit of the man

[1] *La Formation Réligieuse de Jean-Jacques Rousseau.* Par Pierre-Maurice Masson. (Paris : Hachette. Three volumes.)

15

who once thrilled the heart of Europe by stammering forgotten secrets, and whispered to an age flushed and confident with material triumphs that the battle had been won in vain. Rousseau, rightly understood, is no consoling companion for a soldier. What if, after all, the true end of man be those hours of plenary beatitude he spent lying at the bottom of the boat on the Lake of Bienne? What if the old truth is valid still, that man is born free but is everywhere in chains? Let us hope that the dead author was not too keenly conscious of the paradox which claimed him for sacrifice. His death would have been bitter.

From his book we can hardly hazard a judgment. His method would speak against it. Jean-Jacques, as he himself knew only too well, is one of the last great men to be catechised historically, for he was inadequate to the life which is composed of the facts of which histories are made. He had no historical sense; and of a man who has no historical sense no real history can be written. Chronology was meaningless to him because he could recognise no sovereignty of time over himself. With him ends were beginnings. In the third *Dialogue* he tell us—and it is nothing less than the sober truth told by a man who knew himself well—that his works must be read backwards, beginning with the last, by those who would understand him. Indeed, his function was, in a deeper sense than is imagined by those who take the parable called the *Contrat Social* for a solemn treatise of political philosophy, to give the lie to history. In himself he pitted the eternal against the temporal and grew younger with years. He might be known as the man of the second childhood *par excellence*. To the eye

16

of history the effort of his soul was an effort backwards, because the vision of history is focused only for a perspective of progress. On his after-dinner journey to Diderot at Vincennes, Jean-Jacques saw, with the suddenness of intuition, that that progress, amongst whose convinced and cogent prophets he had lived so long, was for him an unsubstantial word. He beheld the soul of man *sub specie æternitatis*. In his vision history and institutions dissolved away. His second childhood had begun.

On such a man the historical method can have no grip. There is, as the French say, no *engrenage*. It points to a certain lack of the subtler kind of understanding to attempt to apply the method; more truly, perhaps, to an unessential interest, which has of late years been imported into French criticism from Germany. The Sorbonne has not, we know, gone unscathed by the disease of documentation for documentation's sake. M. Masson's three volumes leave us with the sense that their author had learnt a method and in his zeal to apply it had lost sight of the momentous question whether Jean-Jacques was a person to whom it might be applied with a prospect of discovery. No one who read Rousseau with a mind free of ulterior motives could have any doubt on the matter. Jean-Jacques is categorical on the point. The Savoyard Vicar was speaking for Jean-Jacques to posterity when he began his profession of faith with the words :—

' Je ne veux argumenter avec vous, ni même de tenter vous convaincre; il me suffit de vous exposer ce que je pense dans la simplicité de mon cœur.

Consultez le vôtre pendant mon discours; c'est tout ce que je vous demande.'

To the extent, therefore, that M. Masson did not respond to this appeal and filled his volumes with information concerning the books Jean-Jacques might have read and a hundred other interesting but only partly relevant things, he did the citizen of Geneva a wrong. The ulterior motive is there, and the faint taste of a thesis in the most modern manner. But the method is saved by the perception which, though it sometimes lacks the perfect keenness of complete understanding, is exquisite enough to suggest the answer to the questions it does not satisfy. Though the environment is lavish the man is not lost.

It is but common piety to seek to understand Jean-Jacques in the way in which he pleaded so hard to be understood. Yet it is now over forty years since a voice of authority told England how it was to regard him. Lord Morley was magisterial and severe, and England obeyed. One feels almost that Jean-Jacques himself would have obeyed if he had been alive. He would have trembled at the stern sentence that his deism was 'a rag of metaphysics floating in a sunshine of sentimentalism,' and he would have whispered that he would try to be good; but, when he heard his *Dialogues* described as the outpourings of a man with persecution mania, he might have rebelled and muttered silently an *Eppur si muove*. We see now that it was a mistake to stand him in the social dock, and that precisely those *Dialogues* which the then Mr Morley so powerfully dismissed contain his plea that the tribunal has no

18

jurisdiction. To his contention that he wrote his books to ease his own soul it might be replied that their publication was a social act which had vast social consequences. But Jean-Jacques might well retort that the fact that his contemporaries and the generation which followed read and judged him in the letter and not in the spirit is no reason why we, at nearly two centuries remove, should do the same.

A great man may justly claim our deference. If Jean-Jacques asks that his last work shall be read first, we are bound, even if we consider it only a quixotic humour, to indulge it. But to those who read the neglected *Dialogues* it will appear a humour no longer. Here is a man who at the end of his days is filled to overflowing with bitterness at the thought that he has been misread and misunderstood. He says to himself : Either he is at bottom of the same nature as other men or he is different. If he is of the same nature, then there must be a malignant plot at work. He has revealed his heart with labour and good faith; not to hear him his fellow-men must have stopped their ears. If he is of another kind than his fellows, then—but he cannot bear the thought. Indeed it is a thought that no man can bear. They are blind because they will not see. He has not asked them to believe that what he says is true; he asks only that they shall believe that he is sincere, sincere in what he says, sincere, above all, when he implores that they should listen to the undertone. He has been ' the painter of nature and the historian of the human heart.'

His critics might have paused to consider why Jean-Jacques, certainly not niggard of self-praise in the *Dialogues*, should have claimed no more for himself than this. He might have claimed, with what in their eyes at least must be good right, to have been pre-eminent in his century as a political philosopher, a novelist, and a theorist of education. Yet to himself he is no more than ' the painter of nature and the historian of the human heart.' Those who would make him more make him less, because they make him other than he declares himself to be. His whole life has been an attempt to be himself and nothing else besides; and all his works have been nothing more and nothing less than his attempt to make his own nature plain to men. Now at the end of his life he has to swallow the bitterness of failure. He has been acclaimed the genius of his age; kings have delighted to honour him, but they have honoured another man. They have not known the true Jean-Jacques. They have taken his parables for literal truth, and he knows why.

' Des êtres si singulièrement constitués doivent nécessairement s'exprimer autrement que les hommes ordinaires. Il est impossible qu'avec des âmes si différemment modifiés ils ne portent pas dans l'expression de leurs sentiments et de leurs idées l'empreinte de ces modifications. Si cette empreinte échappe à ceux qui n'ont aucune notion de cette manière d'être, elle ne peut échapper à ceux qui la connoissent, et qui en sont affectés eux-mêmes. C'est une signe caractéristique auquel les initiés se reconnoissent entre eux; et ce qui donne un grand prix à ce signe, c'est qu'il ne peut se contrefaire, que jamais il n'agit qu'au niveau de sa source, et que, quand il ne part pas du cœur de ceux qui l'imitent, il n'arrive pas non plus aux cœurs faits pour le distinguer; mais sitôt qu'il y parvient, on ne sauroit s'y méprendre; il est vrai dès qu'il est senti.'

At the end of his days he felt that the great labour of his life, which had been to express an intuitive certainty in words which would carry intellectual conviction, had been in vain, and his last words are : ' It is true so soon as it is felt.'

Three pages would tell as much of the essential truth of his ' religious formation ' as three volumes. At Les Charmettes with Mme de Warens, as a boy and as a young man, he had known peace of soul. In Paris, amid the intellectual exaltation and enthusiasms of the Encyclopædists, the memory of his lost peace haunted him like an uneasy conscience. His boyish unquestioning faith disappeared beneath the destructive criticism of the great pioneers of enlightenment and progress. Yet when all had been destroyed the hunger in his heart was still unsatisfied. Underneath his passionate admiration for Diderot smouldered a spark of resentment that he was not understood. They had torn down the fabric of expression into which he had poured the emotion of his immediate certainty as a boy; sometimes with an uplifted, sometimes with a sinking heart he surveyed the ruins. But the certainty that he had once been certain, the memory and the desire of the past peace—this they could not destroy. They could hardly even weaken this element within him, for they did not know that it existed. They were unable to conceive that it could exist. Jean-Jacques himself could give them no clue to its existence; he had no words, and he was still under the spell of the intellectual dogma of his age that words must express definite things. In common with his age he had lost the secret of the infinite persuasion of poetry. So the consciousness that he was different from those who surrounded him, and from those he admired as his masters, took hold of him. He was afraid of his own otherness, as all men are afraid when the first knowledge of their own essential loneliness begins to trouble their depths. The pathos of his struggle to kill the seed of this devastating knowledge is apparent in his declared desire to become ' a polished gentleman.' In the note which he added to his memoir for M. Dupin in 1749 he confesses to this ideal. If only he could become ' one of them,' indistinguishable without and within, he might be delivered from that disquieting sense of tongue-tied queerness in a normal world.

If he cheated himself at all, the deception was brief. The poignant memory of Les Charmettes whispered to him that there was a state of grace in which the hard things were made clear. But he had not yet the courage of his destiny. His consciousness of his separation from his fellows had still to harden into a consciousness of superiority before that courage would come. On the road to Vincennes on an October evening in 1749—M. Masson has fixed the date for us—he read in a news-sheet the question of the Dijon Academy : ' Si le rétablissement des arts et des sciences a contribué à épurer les mœurs ? ' The scales dropped from his eyes and the weight was removed from his tongue. There is no mystery about this ' revelation.' For the first time the question had been put in terms which struck him squarely in the heart. Jean-Jacques made his reply with the stammering honesty of a man of genius wandering in age of talent.

The First Discourse seems to many rhetorical and extravagant. In after days it appeared so to Rousseau himself, and he claimed no more for it than that he had tried to tell the truth. Before he learned that he had won the Dijon prize and that his work had taken Paris by storm, he was surely a prey to terrors lest his Vincennes vision of the non-existence of progress should have been mere madness. The success reassured him. ' Cette faveur du public, nullement brigué, et pour un auteur inconnu, me donna la première assurance véritable de mon talent.' He was, in fact, not ' queer,' but right; and he had seemed to be queer precisely because he was right. Now he had the courage. ' Je suis grossier,' he wrote in the preface to *Narcisse*, ' maussade, impoli par principes; je me fous de tous vous autres gens de cour; je suis un barbare.' There is a touch of exaggeration and bravado in it all. He was still something of the child hallooing in the dark to give himself heart. He clutched hold of material symbols of the freedom he had won, round wig, black stockings, and a living gained by copying music at so much a line. But he did not break with his friends; the ' bear ' suffered himself to be made a lion. He had still a foot in either camp, for though he had the conviction that he was right, he was still fumbling for his words. The memoirs of Madame d'Epinay tell us how in 1754, at dinner at Mlle Quinault's, impotent to reply to the polite atheistical persiflage of the

company, he broke out : ' Et moi, messieurs, je
crois en Dieu. Je sors si vous dites un mot de plus.'
That was not what he meant; neither was the First
Discourse what he meant. He had still to find his
language, and to find his language he had to find his
peace. He was like a twig whirled about in an eddy
of a stream. Suddenly the stream bore him to Geneva,
where he returned to the church which he had left
at Confignon. That, too, was not what he meant.
When he returned from Geneva, Madame d'Epinay
had built him the Ermitage.

In the *Rêveries*, which are mellow with the golden
calm of his discovered peace, he tells how, having
reached the climacteric which he had set at forty
years, he went apart into the solitude of the Ermitage
to inquire into the configuration of his own soul, and
to fix once for all his opinions and his principles.
In the exquisite third *Rêverie* two phrases occur
continually. His purpose was ' to find firm ground '
—' prendre une assiette,'—and his means to this
discovery was ' spiritual honesty '—' bonne foi.'
Rousseau's deep concern was to elucidate the anatomy
of his own soul, but, since he was sincere, he regarded
it as a type of the soul of man. Looking into himself,
he saw that, in spite of all his follies, his weaknesses,
his faintings by the way, his blasphemies against the
spirit, he was good. Therefore he declared : Man
is born good. Looking into himself he saw that he
was free to work out his own salvation, and to find
that solid foundation of peace which he so fervently
desired. Therefore he declared : Man is born free.
To the whisper of les Charmettes that there was a
condition of grace had been added the sterner voice

24

of remorse for his abandoned children, telling him that he had fallen from his high estate.

> 'J'ai fui en vain; partout j'ai retrouvé la Loi.
> Il faut céder enfin! ô porte, il faut admettre
> L'hôte; cœur frémissant, il faut subir le maître,
> Quelqu'un qui soit en moi plus moi-même que
>   moi.'

The noble verse of M. Claudel contains the final secret of Jean-Jacques. He found in himself something more him than himself. Therefore he declared: There is a God. But he sought to work out a logical foundation for these pinnacles of truth. He must translate these luminous convictions of his soul into arguments and conclusions. He could not, even to himself, admit that they were only intuitions; and in the *Contrat Social* he turned the reason to the service of a certainty not her own.

This unremitting endeavour to express an intuitive certainty in intellectual terms lies at the root of the many superficial contradictions in his work, and of the deeper contradiction which forms, as it were, the inward rhythm of his three great books. He seems to surge upwards on a passionate wave of revolutionary ideas, only to sink back into the calm of conservative or quietist conclusions. M. Masson has certainly observed it well.

'Le premier *Discours* anathématise les sciences et les arts, et ne voit le salut que dans les académies; le *Discours sur l'Inégalité* paraît détruire tout autorité, et recommande pourtant "l'obéissance scrupuleuse

aux lois et aux hommes qui en sont les auteurs ":
la *Nouvelle Héloïse* prêche d'abord l'émancipation
sentimentale, et proclame la suprématie des droits
de la passion, mais elle aboutit à exalter la fidelité
conjugale, à consolider les grands devoirs familiaux
et sociaux. Le Vicaire Savoyard nous reserve la
même surprise.'

To the revolutionaries of his age he was a renegade
and a reactionary; to the Conservatives, a subversive
charlatan. Yet he was in truth only a man stricken
by the demon of ' la bonne foi,' and, like many men
devoured by the passion of spiritual honesty, in his
secret heart he believed in his similitude to Christ.
' Je ne puis pas souffrir les tièdes,' he wrote to Madame
Latour in 1762, ' quiconque ne se passionne pas pour
moi n'est pas digne de moi.' There is no mistaking
the accent, and it sounds more plainly still in the
Dialogues. He, too, was persecuted for righteousness'
sake, because he, too, proclaimed that the kingdom
of heaven was within men.

And what, indeed, have material things to do
with the purification and the peace of the soul ?
World-shattering arguments and world-preserving
conclusions—this is the inevitable paradox which
attends the attempt to record truth seen by the eye of
the soul in the language of the market-place. The
eloquence and the inspiration may descend upon the
man so that he writes believing that all men will
understand. He wakes in the morning and he is
afraid, not of his own words whose deeper truth he
does not doubt, but of the incapacity of mankind to
understand him. They will read in the letter what

was written in the spirit; their eyes will see the words, but their ears will be stopped to the music. The *mystique*, as Péguy would have said, will be degraded into *politique*. To guard himself against this unhallowed destiny, at the last Rousseau turns with decision and in the language of his day rewrites the hard saying, that the things which are Cæsar's shall be rendered unto Cæsar.

In the light of this necessary truth all the contradictions which have been discovered in Rousseau's work fade away. That famous confusion concerning ' the natural man,' whom he presents to us now as a historic fact, now as an ideal, took its rise, not in the mind of Jean-Jacques, but in the minds of his critics. The *Contrat Social* is a parable of the soul of man, like the *Republic* of Plato. The truth of the human soul is its implicit perfection; to that reality material history is irrelevant, because the anatomy of the soul is eternal. And as for the nature of this truth, ' it is true so soon as it is felt.' When the Savoyard Vicar, after accepting all the destructive criticism of religious dogma, turned to the Gospel story with the immortal ' Ce n'est pas ainsi qu'on invente,' he was only anticipating what Jean-Jacques was to say of himself before his death, that there was a sign in his work which could not be imitated, and which acted only at the level of its source. We may call Jean-Jacques religious because we have no other word; but the word would be more truly applied to the reverence felt towards such a man than to his own emotion. He was driven to speak of God by the habit of his childhood and the deficiency of a language shaped by the intellect and not by the soul. But his deity was

27

one whom neither the Catholic nor the Reformed Church could accept, for He was truly a God who does not dwell in temples made with hands. The respect he owed to God, said the Vicar, was such that he could affirm nothing of Him. And, again, still more profoundly, he said, ' He is to our souls what our soul is to our body.' That is the mystical utterance of a man who was no mystic, but of one who found his full communion in the beatific *dolce far niente* of the Lake of Bienne. Jean-Jacques was set apart from his generation, because, like Malvolio, he thought highly of the soul and in nowise approved the conclusions of his fellows; and he was fortunate to the last, in spite of what some are pleased to call his madness (which was indeed only his flaming and uncomprehending indignation at the persecution inevitably meted out by those who have only a half truth to one who has the whole), because he enjoyed the certainty that his high appraisement of the soul was justified.

[MARCH, 1918.

The Poetry of Edward Thomas

WE believe that when we are old and we turn back to look among the ruins with which our memory will be strewn for the evidence of life which disaster could not kill, we shall find it in the poems of Edward Thomas.[1] They will appear like the faint, indelible writing of a palimpsest over which in our hours of exaltation and bitterness more resonant, yet less enduring, words were inscribed; or they will be like a phial discovered in the ashes of what was once a mighty city. There will be the triumphal arch standing proudly; the very tombs of the dead will seem to share its monumental magnificence. Yet we will turn from them all, from the victory and sorrow alike, to this faintly gleaming bubble of glass that will hold captive the phantasm of a fragrance of the soul. By it some dumb and doubtful knowledge will be evoked to tremble on the edge of our minds. We shall reach back, under its spell, beyond the larger impulses of a resolution and a resignation which will have become a part of history, to something less solid and more permanent over which they passed and which they could not disturb.

Our consciousness will have its record. The tradition of England in battle has its testimony; our less traditional despairs will be compassed about by a crowd of witnesses. But it might so nearly have been in vain that we should seek an echo of that which smiled at the conclusions of our consciousness. The

[1] *Last Poems.* By Edward Thomas. (Selwyn & Blount.)

subtler faiths might so easily have fled through our harsh fingers. When the sound of the bugles died, having crowned reveillé with the equal challenge of the last post, how easily we might have been persuaded that there was a silence, if there had not been one whose voice rose only so little above that of the winds and trees and the life of undertone we share with them as to make us first doubt the silence and then lend an ear to the incessant pulses of which it is composed. The infinite and infinitesimal vague happinesses and immaterial alarms, terrors and beauties scared by the sound of speech, memories and forgettings that the touch of memory itself crumbles into dust—this very texture of the life of the soul might have been a gray background over which tumultuous existence passed unheeding had not Edward Thomas so painfully sought the angle from which it appears, to the eye of eternity, as the enduring warp of the more gorgeous woof.

The emphasis sinks; the stresses droop away. To exacter knowledge less charted and less conquerable certainties succeed; truths that somehow we cannot make into truths, and that have therefore some strange mastery over us; laws of our common substance which we cannot make human but only humanise; loyalties we do not recognise and dare not disregard; beauties which deny communion with our beautiful, and yet compel our souls. So the sedge-warbler's

'Song that lacks all words, all melody,
All sweetness almost, was dearer then to me
Than sweetest voice that sings in tune sweet
    words.'

Not that the unheard melodies were sweeter than the heard to this dead poet. We should be less confident of his quality if he had not been, both in his knowledge and his hesitations, the child of his age. Because he was this, the melodies were heard; but they were not sweet. They made the soul sensible of attachments deeper than the conscious mind's ideals, whether of beauty or goodness. Not to something above but to something beyond are we chained, for all that we forget our fetters, or by some queer trick of self-hallucination turn them into golden crowns. But perhaps the finer task of our humanity is to turn our eyes calmly into ' the dark backward and abysm ' not of time, but of the eternal present on whose pinnacle we stand.

> ' I have mislaid the key. I sniff the spray
> And think of nothing; I see and hear nothing;
> Yet seem, too, to be listening, lying in wait
> For what I should, yet never can, remember.
> No garden appears, no path, no child beside,
> Neither father nor mother, nor any playmate;
> Only an avenue, dark, nameless without end.'

So, it seems, a hundred years have found us out. We come no longer trailing clouds of glory. We are that which we are, less and more than our strong ancestors; less, in that our heritage does not descend from on high, more, in that we know ourselves for less. Yet our chosen spirit is not wholly secure in his courage. He longs not merely to know in what un-differentiated oneness his roots are fixed, but to discover it beautiful. Not even yet is it sufficient to

have a premonition of the truth; the truth must wear
a familiar colour.

> ' This heart, some fraction of me, happily
> Floats through the window even now to a tree
> Down in the misting, dim-lit, quiet vale,
> Not like a peewit that returns to wail
> For something it has lost, but like a dove
> That slants unswerving to its home and love.
> There I find my rest, and through the dark air
> Flies what yet lives in me.   Beauty is there.'

Beauty, yes, perhaps; but beautiful by virtue of its
coincidence with the truth, as there is beauty in those
lines securer and stronger far than the melody of their
cadence, because they tell of a loyalty of man's being
which, being once made sensible of it, he cannot
gainsay.   Whence we all come, whither we must all
make our journey, there is home indeed.   But necessity, not remembered delights, draws us thither.   That
which we must obey is our father if we will; but let
us not delude ourselves into the expectation of kindness and the fatted calf, any more than we dare believe
that the love which moves the sun and the other stars
has in it any charity.   We may be, we are, the children
of the universe; but we have ' neither father nor
mother nor any playmate.'

And Edward Thomas knew this.   The knowledge
should be the common property of the poetry of our
time, marking it off from what went before and from
what will come after.   We believe that it will be found
to be so; and that the presence of this knowledge,
and the quality which this knowledge imparts, makes

The Poetry of Edward Thomas

Edward Thomas more than one among his contemporaries. He is their chief. He challenges other regions in the hinterland of our souls. Yet how shall we describe the narrowness of the line which divides his province from theirs, or the only half-conscious subtlety of the gesture with which he beckons us aside from trodden and familiar paths ? The difference, the sense of departure, is perhaps most apparent in this, that he knows his beauty is not beautiful, and his home no home at all.

> ' This is my grief. That land,
> My home, I have never seen.
> No traveller tells of it,
> However far he has been.
>
> ' And could I discover it
> I fear my happiness there,
> Or my pain, might be dreams of return
> To the things that were.'

Great poetry stands in this, that it expresses man's allegiance to his destiny. In every age the great poet triumphs in all that he knows of necessity; thus he is the world made vocal. Other generations of men may know more, but their increased knowledge will not diminish from the magnificence of the music which he has made for the spheres. The known truth alters from age to age; but the thrill of the recognition of the truth stands fast for all our human eternity. Year by year the universe grows vaster, and man, by virtue of the growing brightness of his little lamp, sees himself more and more as a child born in the midst of

33

a dark forest, and finds himself less able to claim the obeisance of the all. Yet if he would be a poet, and not a harper of threadbare tunes, he must at each step in the downward passing from his sovereignty, recognise what is and celebrate it as what must be. Thus he regains, by another path, the supremacy which he has forsaken.

Edward Thomas's poetry has the virtue of this recognition. It may be said that his universe was not vaster but smaller than the universe of the past, for its bounds were largely those of his own self. It is, even in material fact, but half true. None more closely than he regarded the living things of earth in all their quarters. 'After Rain' is, for instance, a very catalogue of the texture of nature's visible garment, freshly put on, down to the little ash-leaves

'. . . thinly spread
In the road, like little black fish, inlaid
As if they played.'

But it is true that these objects of vision were but the occasion of the more profound discoveries within the region of his own soul. There he discovered vastness and illimitable vistas; found himself to be an eddy in the universal flux, driven whence and whither he knew not, conscious of perpetual instability, the meeting place of mighty impacts of which only the farthest ripple agitates the steady moonbeam of the waking mind. In a sense he did no more than to state what he found, sometimes in the more familiar language of beauties lost, mourned for lost, and irrecoverable.

34

' The simple lack
Of her is more to me
Than other's presence,
Whether life splendid be
Or utter black.

' I have not seen,
I have no news of her;
I can tell only
She is not here, but there
She might have been.

' She is to be kissed
Only perhaps by me;
She may be seeking
Me and no other; she
May not exist.'

That search lies nearer to the norm of poetry. We might register its wistfulness, praise the appealing nakedness of its diction and pass on. If that were indeed the culmination of Edward Thomas's poetical quest, he would stand securely enough with others of his time. But he reaches further. In the verses on his ' home,' which we have already quoted, he passes beyond these limits. He has still more to tell of the experience of the soul fronting its own infinity:—

' So memory made
Parting to-day a double pain:
First because it was parting; next
Because the ill it ended vexed
And mocked me from the past again.

Not as what had been remedied
Had I gone on,—not that, ah no!
But as itself no longer woe.'

There speaks a deep desire born only of deep knowledge. Only those who have been struck to the
heart by a sudden awareness of the incessant not-
being which is all we hold of being, know the longing
to arrest the movement even at the price of the per-
petuation of their pain. So it was that the moments
which seemed to come to him free from the infirmity
of becoming haunted and held him most.

' Often I had gone this way before,
But now it seemed I never could be
And never had been anywhere else.'

To cheat the course of time, which is only the name
with which we strive to cheat the flux of things, and
to anchor the soul to something that was not instantly
engulfed—
' In the undefiled
Abyss of what can never be again.'

Sometimes he looked within himself for the monition
which men have felt as the voice of the eternal memory;
sometimes, like Keats, but with none of the intoxica-
tion of Keats's sense of a sharing in victory, he grasped
at the recurrence of natural things, ' the pure thrush
word,' repeated every spring, the law of wheeling
rooks, or to the wind ' that was old when the gods
were young,' as in this profoundly typical sensing of
' A New House.'

36

The Poetry of Edward Thomas

' All was foretold me; naught
      Could I foresee;
  But I learned how the wind would sound
      After these things should be.'

But he could not rest even there.   There was,
indeed, no anchorage in the enduring to be found by
one so keenly aware of the flux within the soul itself.
The most powerful, the most austerely imagined poem
in this book is that entitled 'The Other,' which, apart
from its intrinsic appeal, shows that Edward Thomas
had something at least of the power to create the
myth which is the poet's essential means of triangulat-
ing the unknown of his emotion.   Had he lived to
perfect himself in the use of this instrument, he might
have been a great poet indeed.   ' The Other ' tells
of his pursuit of himself, and how he overtook his
soul.

  ' And now I dare not follow after
    Too close.   I try to keep in sight,
  Dreading his frown and worse his laughter,
  I steal out of the wood to light;
  I see the swift shoot from the rafter
  By the window: ere I alight
  I wait and hear the starlings wheeze
  And nibble like ducks: I wait his flight.
  He goes: I follow: no release
  Until he ceases.   Then I also shall cease.'

No; not a great poet, will be the final sentence,
when the palimpsest is read with the calm and un-
divided attention that is its due, but one who had
many (and among them the chief) of the qualities of

37

a great poet. Edward Thomas was like a musician who noted down themes that summon up forgotten expectations. Whether the genius to work them out to the limits of their scope and implication was in him we do not know. The life of literature was a hard master to him; and perhaps the opportunity he would eagerly have grasped was denied him by circumstance. But, if his compositions do not, his themes will never fail—of so much we are sure—to awaken unsuspected echoes even in unsuspecting minds.   [JANUARY, 1919.

Mr Yeats's Swan Song

In the preface to *The Wild Swans at Coole*,[1] Mr W. B. Yeats speaks of ' the phantasmagoria through which alone I can express my convictions about the world.' The challenge could hardly be more direct. At the threshold we are confronted with a legend upon the door-post which gives us the essential plan of all that we shall find in the house if we enter in. There are, it is true, a few things capable of common use, verses written in the seeming-strong vernacular of literary Dublin, as it were a hospitable bench placed outside the door. They are indeed inside the house, but by accident or for temporary shelter. They do not, as the phrase goes, belong to the scheme, for they are direct transcriptions of the common reality, whether found in the sensible world or the emotion of the mind. They are, from Mr Yeats's angle of vision (as indeed from our own), essentially *vers d'occasion*.

The poet's high and passionate argument must be sought elsewhere, and precisely in his expression of his convictions about the world. And here, on the poet's word and the evidence of our search, we shall find phantasmagoria, ghostly symbols of a truth which cannot be otherwise conveyed, at least by Mr Yeats. To this, in itself, we make no demur. The poet, if he is a true poet, is driven to approach the highest reality he can apprehend. He cannot transcribe it simply because he does not possess the

[1] *The Wild Swans at Coole.* By W. B. Yeats. (Macmillan.)

necessary apparatus of knowledge, and because if he did possess it his passion would flag. It is not often that Spinoza can disengage himself to write as he does at the beginning of the third book of the Ethics, nor could Lucretius often kindle so great a fire in his soul as that which made his material incandescent in *Æneadum genetrix.* Therefore the poet turns to myth as a foundation upon which he can explicate his imagination. He may take his myth from legend or familiar history, or he may create one for himself anew; but the function it fulfils is always the same. It supplies the elements with which he can build the structure of his parable, upon which he can make it elaborate enough to convey the multitudinous reactions of his soul to the world.

But between myths and phantasmagoria there is a great gulf. The structural possibilities of the myth depend upon its intelligibility. The child knows upon what drama, played in what world, the curtain will rise when he hears the trumpet-note: ' Of man's first disobedience. . . .' And, even when the poet turns from legend and history to create his own myth, he must make one whose validity is visible, if he is not to be condemned to the sterility of a coterie. The lawless and fantastic shapes of his own imagination need, even for their own perfect embodiment, the discipline of the common perception. The phantoms of the individual brain, left to their own waywardness, lose all solidity and become like primary forms of life, instead of the penultimate forms they should be. For the poet himself must move securely among his visions; they must be not less certain and steadfast than men are. To anchor them he needs intelligible myth. Nothing less than a supremely great genius can save him if he ventures into the vast without a landmark visible to other eyes than his own. Blake had a supremely great genius and was saved in part. The masculine vigour of his passion gave stability to the figures of his imagination. They are heroes because they are made to speak like heroes. Even in Blake's most recondite work there is always the moment when the clouds are parted and we recognise the austere and awful countenances of gods. The phantasmagoria of the dreamer have been mastered by the sheer creative will of the poet. Like Jacob, he wrestled until the going down of the sun with his angel and would not let him go.

The effort which such momentary victories demand is almost superhuman; yet to possess the power to exert it is the sole condition upon which a poet may plunge into the world of phantasms. Mr Yeats has too little of the power to vindicate himself from the charge of idle dreaming. He knows the problem; perhaps he has also known the struggle. But the very terms in which he suggests it to us subtly convey a sense of impotence:—

> Hands, do what you're bid;
> Bring the balloon of the mind
> That bellies and drags in the wind
> Into its narrow shed.

The languor and ineffectuality of the image tell us clearly how the poet has failed in his larger task; its exactness, its precise expression of an ineffectuality made conscious and condoned, bears equal witness to the poet's minor probity. He remains an artist by determination, even though he returns downcast and defeated from the great quest of poetry. We were inclined at first, seeing those four lines enthroned in majestic isolation on a page, to find in them evidence of an untoward conceit. Subsequently they have seemed to reveal a splendid honesty. Although it has little mysterious and haunting beauty, *The Wild Swans at Coole* is indeed a swan song. It is eloquent of final defeat; the following of a lonely path has ended in the poet's sinking exhausted in a wilderness of gray. Not even the regret is passionate; it is pitiful.

> ' I am worn out with dreams,
> A weather-worn, marble triton
> Among the streams;
> And all day long I look
> Upon this lady's beauty
> As though I had found in book
> A pictured beauty,
> Pleased to have filled the eyes
> Or the discerning ears,
> Delighted to be but wise,
> For men improve with the years;
> And yet, and yet
> Is this my dream, or the truth ?
> O would that we had met
> When I had my burning youth;
> But I grow old among dreams,
> A weather-worn, marble triton
> Among the streams.'

Mr Yeats's Swan Song

It is pitiful because, even now in spite of all his honesty, the poet mistakes the cause of his sorrow. He is worn out not with dreams, but with the vain effort to master them and submit them to his own creative energy. He has not subdued them nor built a new world from them; he has merely followed them like will-o'-the-wisps away from the world he knew. Now, possessing neither world, he sits by the edge of a barren road that vanishes into a no-man's land, where is no future, and whence there is no way back to the past.

> ' My country is Kiltartan Cross,
> My countrymen Kiltartan's poor;
> No likely end could bring them loss
> Or leave them happier than before.'

It may be that Mr Yeats has succumbed to the malady of a nation. We do not know whether such things are possible; we must consider him only in and for himself. From this angle we can regard him only as a poet whose creative vigour has failed him when he had to make the highest demands upon it. His sojourn in the world of the imagination, far from enriching his vision, has made it infinitely tenuous. Of this impoverishment, as of all else that has overtaken him, he is agonisedly aware.

> ' I would find by the edge of that water
> The collar-bone of a hare,
> Worn thin by the lapping of the water,
> And pierce it through with a gimlet, and stare

43

> At the old bitter world where they marry in
> churches,
> And laugh over the untroubled water
> At all who marry in churches,
> Through the white thin bone of a hare.'

Nothing there remains of the old bitter world, which for all its bitterness is a full world also; but nothing remains of the sweet world of imagination. Mr Yeats has made the tragic mistake of thinking that to contemplate it was sufficient. Had he been a great poet he would have made it his own, by forcing it into the fetters of speech. By re-creating it, he would have made it permanent; he would have built landmarks to guide him always back to where the effort of his last discovery had ended. But now there remains nothing but a handful of the symbols with which he was content:—

> 'A Sphinx with woman breast and lion paw,
> A Buddha, hand at rest,
> Hand lifted up that blest;
> And right between these two a girl at play.'

These are no more than the dry bones in the valley of Ezekiel, and, alas! there is no prophetic fervour to make them live.

Whether Mr Yeats, by some grim fatality, mistook his phantasmagoria for the product of the creative imagination, or whether (as we prefer to believe) he made an effort to discipline them to his poetic purpose and failed, we cannot certainly say. Of this, however, we are certain, that somehow, somewhere, there

44

has been disaster. He is empty, now. He has the apparatus of enchantment, but no potency in his soul. He is forced to fall back upon the artistic honesty which has never forsaken him. That it is an insufficient reserve let this passage show:—

> ' For those that love the world serve it in action,
> Grow rich, popular, and full of influence,
> And should they paint or write still it is action:
> The struggle of the fly in marmalade.
> The rhetorician would deceive his neighbours,
> The sentimentalist himself; while art
> Is but a vision of reality. . . .'

Mr Yeats is neither rhetorician nor sentimentalist. He is by structure and impulse an artist. But structure and impulse are not enough. Passionate apprehension must be added to them. Because this is lacking in Mr Yeats those lines, concerned though they are with things he holds most dear, are prose and not poetry. [APRIL, 1919.

The Wisdom of Anatole France

How few are the wise writers who remain to us ?
They are so few that it seems, at moments, that
wisdom, like justice of old, is withdrawing from the
world, and that when their fullness of years is accomplished, as, alas ! it soon must be, the wise men who
will leave us will have been the last of their kind.   It
is true that something akin to wisdom, or rather a
quality whose outward resemblance to wisdom can
deceive all but the elect, will emerge from the ruins of
war; but true wisdom is not created out of the
catastrophic shock of disillusionment.   An unexpected
disaster is always held to be in some sort undeserved.
Yet the impulse to rail at destiny, be it never so
human, is not wise.   Wisdom is not bitter; at worst
it is bitter-sweet, and bitter-sweet is the most subtle
and lingering savour of all.

Let us not say in our haste, that without wisdom
we are lost.   Wisdom is, after all, but one attitude to
life among many.   It happens to be the one which
will stand the hardest wear, because it is prepared for
all ill-usage.   But hard wear is not the only purpose
which an attitude may serve.   We may demand of an
attitude that it should enable us to exact the utmost
from ourselves.   To refuse to accommodate oneself
to the angularities of life or to make provision before-
hand for its catastrophes is, indeed, folly; but it may
be a divine folly.   It is, at all events, a folly to which
poets incline.   But poets are not wise; indeed, the
poetry of true wisdom is a creation which can, at the

46

best, be but dimly imagined. Perhaps, of them all, Lucretius had the largest inkling of what such poetry might be; but he disqualified himself by an aptitude for ecstasy, which made his poetry superb and his wisdom of no account. To acquiesce is wise; to be ecstatic in acquiescence is not to have acquiesced at all. It is to have identified oneself with an imagined power against whose manifestations, in those moments when no ecstasy remains, one rebels. It is a megalomania, a sublime self-deception, a heroic attempt to project the soul on to the side of destiny, and to believe ourselves the masters of those very powers which have overwhelmed us.

Whether the present generation will produce great poetry, we do not know. We are tolerably certain that it will not produce wise men. It is too conscious of defeat and too embittered to be wise. Some may seek that ecstasy of seeming acquiescence of which we have spoken; others, who do not endeavour to escape the pain by plunging the barb deeper, may try to shake the dust of life from off their feet. Neither will be wise. But precisely because they are not wise, they will seek the company of wise men. Their own attitude will not wear. The ecstasy will fail, the will to renunciation falter; the gray reality which permits no one to escape it altogether will filter like a mist into the vision and the cell. Then they will turn to the wise men. They will find comfort in the smile to which they could not frame their own lips, and discover in it more sympathy than they could hope for.

Among the wise men whom they will surely most frequent will be Anatole France. His company is

47

constant; his attitude durable. There is no undertone of anguish in his work like that which gives such poignant and haunting beauty to Tchehov. He has never suffered himself to be so involved in life as to be maimed by it. But the price he has paid for his safety has been a renunciation of experience. Only by being involved in life, perhaps only by being maimed by it, could he have gained that bitterness of knowledge which is the enemy of wisdom. Not that Anatole France made a deliberate renunciation: no man of his humanity would of his own will turn aside. It was instinct which guided him into a sequestered path, which ran equably by the side of the road of alternate exaltation and catastrophe which other men of equal genius must travel. Therefore he has seen men as it were in profile against the sky, but never face to face. Their runnings, their stumblings and their gesticulations are a tumultuous portion of the landscape rather than symbols of an intimate and personal possibility. They lend a baroque enchantment to the scene.

So it is that in all the characters of Anatole France's work which are not closely modelled upon his own idiosyncrasy there is something of the marionette. They are not the less charming for that; nor do they lack a certain logic, but it is not the logic of personality. They are embodied comments upon life, but they do not live. And there is for Anatole France, while he creates them, and for us, while we read about them, no reason why they should live. For living, in the accepted sense, is an activity impossible without indulging many illusions; and fervently to sympathise with characters engaged in

48

the activity demands that their author should participate in the illusions. He, too, must be surprised at the disaster which he himself has proved inevitable. It is not enough that he should pity them; he must share in their effort, and be discomfited at their discomfiture.

Such exercises of the soul are impossible to a real acquiescence, which cannot even permit itself the inspiration of the final illusion that the wreck of human hopes, being ordained, is beautiful. The man who acquiesces is condemned to stand apart and contemplate a puppet-show with which he can never really sympathise.

'De toutes les définitions de l'homme la plus mauvaise me paraît celle qui en fait un animal raisonnable. Je ne me vante pas excessivement en me donnant pour doué de plus de raison que la plupart de ceux de mes semblables que j'ai vus de près ou dont j'ai connu l'histoire. La raison habite rarement les âmes communes, et bien plus rarement encore les grands esprits. . . . J'appelle raisonnable celui qui accorde sa raison particulière avec la raison universelle, de manière à n'être jamais trop surpris de ce qui arrive et à s'y accommoder tant bien que mal; j'appelle raisonnable celui qui, observant le désordre de la nature et la folie humaine, ne s'obstine point à y voir de l'ordre et de la sagesse; j'appelle raisonnable enfin celui qui ne s'efforce pas de l'être.'

The chasm between living and being wise (which is to be *raisonnable*) is manifest. The condition of living is to be perpetually surprised, incessantly indignant or exultant, at what happens. To bridge the chasm there is for the wise man only one way. He must cast back in his memory to the time when he, too, was surprised and indignant. No man is, after all, born wise, though he may be born with an instinct for wisdom. Thus Anatole France touches us most nearly when he describes his childhood. The innocent, wayward, positive, romantic little Pierre Nozière[1] is a human being to a degree to which no other figures in the master's comedy of unreason are. And it is evident that Anatole France himself finds him by far the most attractive of them all. He can almost persuade himself, at moments, that he still is the child he was, as in the exquisite story of how, when he had been to a truly royal chocolate shop, he attempted to reproduce its splendours in play. At one point his invention and his memory failed him, and he turned to his mother to ask: ' Est-ce celui qui vend ou celui qui achète qui donne de l'argent ? '

' Je ne devais jamais connaître le prix de l'argent. Tel j'étais à trois ans ou trois ans et demi dans le cabinet tapissé de boutons de roses, tel je restai jusqu'à la vieillesse, qui m'est légère, comme elle l'est à toutes les âmes exemptes d'avarice et d'orgueil. Non, maman, je n'ai jamais connu le prix de l'argent. Je ne le connais pas encore, ou plutôt je le connais trop bien.'

To know a thing too well is by worlds removed from not to know it at all, and Anatole France does not elsewhere similarly attempt to indulge the illusion

[1] *Le Petit Pierre.* Par Anatole France. (Paris : Calmann-Lévy.)

of unbroken innocence. He who refused to put a mark of interrogation after ' What is God,' in defiance of his mother, because he knew, now has to restrain himself from putting one after everything he writes or thinks. ' Ma pauvre mère, si elle vivait, me dirait peut-être que maintenant j'en mets trop.' Yes, Anatole France is wise, and far removed from childish follies. And, perhaps, it is precisely because of his wisdom that he can so exactly discern the enchantment of his childhood. So few men grow up. The majority remain hobbledehoys throughout life; all the disabilities and none of the unique capacities of childhood remain. There are a few who, in spite of all experience, retain both; they are the poets and the *grands esprits*. There are fewer still who learn utterly to renounce childish things; and they are the wise men.

' Je suis une autre personne que l'enfant dont je parle. Nous n'avons plus en commun, lui et moi, un atome de substance ni de pensée. Maintenant qu'il m'est devenu tout à fait étranger, je puis en sa compagnie me distraire de la mienne. Je l'aime, moi qui ne m'aime ni ne me haïs. Il m'est doux de vivre en pensée les jours qu'il vivait et je souffre de respirer l'air du temps où nous sommes.'

Not otherwise is it with us and Anatole France. We may have little in common with his thought— the community we often imagine comes of self-deception—but it is sweet for us to inhabit his mind for a while. His touch is potent to soothe our fitful fevers. [APRIL, 1919.

Gerard Manley Hopkins

MODERN poetry, like the modern consciousness of which it is the epitome, seems to stand irresolute at a crossways with no signpost. It is hardly conscious of its own indecision, which it manages to conceal from itself by insisting that it is lyrical, whereas it is merely impressionist. The value of impressions depends upon the quality of the mind which receives and renders them, and to be lyrical demands at least as firm a temper of the mind, as definite and unfaltering a general direction, as to be epic. Roughly speaking, the present poetical fashion may, with a few conspicuous exceptions, be described as poetry without tears. The poet may assume a hundred personalities in as many poems, or manifest a hundred influences, or he may work a single sham personality threadbare or render piecemeal an undigested influence. What he may not do, or do only at the risk of being unfashionable, is to attempt what we may call, for the lack of a better word, the logical progression of an *œuvre*. One has no sense of the rhythm of an achievement. There is an output of scraps, which are scraps, not because they are small, but because one scrap stands in no organic relation to another in the poet's work. Instead of lending each other strength, they betray each other's weakness.

Yet the organic progression for which we look, generally in vain, is not peculiar to poetic genius of the highest rank. If it were, we might be accused of mere querulousness. The rhythm of personality

52

is hard, indeed, to achieve. The simple mind and the single outlook are now too rare to be considered as near possibilities, while the task of tempering a mind to a comprehensive adequacy to modern experience is not an easy one. The desire to escape and the desire to be lost in life were probably never so intimately associated as they are now; and it is a little preposterous to ask a moth fluttering round a candle-flame to see life steadily and see it whole. We happen to have been born into an age without perspective; hence our idolatry for the one living poet and prose writer who has it and comes, or appears to come, from another age. But another rhythm is possible. No doubt it would be mistaken to consider this rhythm as in fact wholly divorced from the rhythm of personality; it probably demands at least a minimum of personal coherence in its possessor. For critical purposes, however, they are distinct. This second and subsidiary rhythm is that of technical progression. The single pursuit of even the most subordinate artistic intention gives unity, significance, mass to a poet's work. When Verlaine declares ' de la musique avant toute chose,' we know where we are. And we know this not in the obvious sense of expecting his verse to be predominantly musical; but in the more important sense of desiring to take a man seriously who declares for anything ' avant toute chose.'

It is the ' avant toute chose ' that matters, not as a profession of faith—we do not greatly like professions of faith—but as the guarantee of the universal in the particular, of the *dianoia* in the episode. It is the ' avant toute chose ' that we chiefly miss in modern

poetry and modern society and in their quaint concatenations. It is the ' avant toute chose ' that leads
us to respect both Mr Hardy and Mr Bridges, though
we give all our affection to one of them. It is the
' avant toute chose ' that compels us to admire the
poems of Gerard Manley Hopkins[1]; it is the ' avant
toute chose ' in his work, which, as we believe, would
have condemned him to obscurity to-day, if he had
not (after many years) had Mr Bridges, who was his
friend, to stand sponsor and the Oxford University
Press to stand the racket. Apparently Mr Bridges
himself is something of our opinion, for his introductory sonnet ends on a disdainful note:—

> ' Go forth: amidst our chaffinch flock display
> Thy plumage of far wonder and heavenward
>   flight! '

It is from a sonnet written by Hopkins to Mr
Bridges that we take the most concise expression of
his artistic intention, for the poet's explanatory
preface is not merely technical, but is written in a
technical language peculiar to himself. Moreover,
its scope is small; the sonnet tells us more in two
lines than the preface in four pages.

> ' O then if in my lagging lines you miss
> The roll, the rise, the carol, the creation. . . .'

There is his ' avant toute chose.' Perhaps it seems
very like ' de la musique.' But it tells us more about

---

[1] *Poems of Gerard Manley Hopkins.* Edited with notes by Robert
Bridges. (Oxford : University Press.)

Hopkins's music than Verlaine's line told us about his. This music is of a particular kind, not the 'sanglots du violon,' but pre-eminently the music of song, the music most proper to lyrical verse. If one were to seek in English the lyrical poem to which Hopkins's definition could be most fittingly applied, one would find Shelley's ' Skylark.' A technical progression onwards from the ' Skylark ' is accordingly the main line of Hopkins's poetical evolution. There are other, stranger threads interwoven; but this is the chief. Swinburne, rightly enough if the intention of true song is considered, appears hardly to have existed for Hopkins, though he was his contemporary. There is an element of Keats in his epithets, a half-echo in ' whorlèd ear ' and ' lark-charmèd '; there is an aspiration after Milton's architectonic in the construction of the later sonnets and the most lucid of the fragments, ' Epithalamion.' But the central point of departure is the ' Skylark.' The ' May Magnificat ' is evidence of Hopkins's achievement in the direct line:—

> ' Ask of her, the mighty mother:
> Her reply puts this other
> Question: What is Spring?—
> Growth in everything—
>
> Flesh and fleece, fur and feather,
> Grass and greenworld all together;
> Star-eyed strawberry-breasted
> Throstle above her nested
> Cluster of bugle-blue eggs thin
> Forms and warms the life within. . . .

> . . . When drop-of-blood-and-foam-dapple
> Bloom lights the orchard-apple,
> And thicket and thorp are merry
> With silver-surfèd cherry,
>
> And azuring-over graybell makes
> Wood banks and brakes wash wet like lakes,
> And magic cuckoo-call
> Caps, clears, and clinches all. . . .'

That is the primary element manifested in one of its simplest, most recognisable, and some may feel most beautiful forms. But a melody so simple, though it is perhaps the swiftest of which the English language is capable without the obscurity which comes of the drowning of sense in sound, did not satisfy Hopkins. He aimed at complex internal harmonies, at a counterpoint of rhythm; for this more complex element he coined an expressive word of his own:—

' But as air, melody, is what strikes me most of all in music and design in painting, so design, pattern, or what I am in the habit of calling *inscape* is what I above all aim at in poetry.'

Here, then, in so many words, is Hopkins's ' avant toute chose ' at a higher level of elaboration. ' Inscape ' is still, in spite of the apparent differentiation, musical; but a quality of formalism seems to have entered with the specific designation. With formalism comes rigidity; and in this case the rigidity is bound to overwhelm the sense. For the relative constant in the composition of poetry is the law of language which admits only a certain amount of adaptation. Musical design must be subordinate to it, and the poet should be aware that even in speaking of musical design he is indulging a metaphor. Hopkins admitted this, if we may judge by his practice, only towards the end of his life. There is no escape by sound from the meaning of the posthumous sonnets, though we may hesitate to pronounce whether this directness was due to a modification of his poetical principles or to the urgency of the content of the sonnets, which, concerned with a matter of life and death, would permit no obscuring of their sense for musical reasons.

> ' I wake and feel the fell of dark, not day.
> What hours, O what black hours we have spent
> This night! what sights you, heart, saw; ways
>   you went!
> And more must in yet longer light's delay.
>   With witness I speak this. But where I say
> Hours I mean years, mean life. And my lament
> Is cries countless, cries like dead letters sent
> To dearest him that lives, alas! away.'

There is compression, but not beyond immediate comprehension; music, but a music of overtones; rhythm, but a rhythm which explicates meaning and makes it more intense.

Between the ' May Magnificat ' and these sonnets is the bulk of Hopkins's poetical work and his peculiar achievement. Perhaps it could be regarded as a phase in his evolution towards the ' more balanced and Miltonic style ' which he hoped for, and of which

57

the posthumous sonnets are precursors; but the attempt to see him from this angle would be perverse. Hopkins was not the man to feel, save on exceptional occasions, that urgency of content of which we have spoken. The communication of thought was seldom the dominant impulse of his creative moment, and it is curious how simple his thought often proves to be when the obscurity of his language has been penetrated. Musical elaboration is the chief characteristic of his work, and for this reason what seem to be the strangest of his experiments are his most essential achievement. So, for instance, 'The Golden Echo':—

> ' Spare!
> There is one, yes, I have one (Hush there!);
> Only not within seeing of sun,
> Not within the singeing of the strong sun,
> Tall sun's tingeing, or treacherous the tainting
>   of the earth's air,
> Somewhere else where there is, ah, well, where!
>   one,
> One. Yes, I can tell such a key, I do know such
>   a place,
> Where, whatever's prized and passes of us,
>   everything that's fresh and fast flying of
>   us, seems to us sweet of us and swiftly away
>   with, done away with, undone,
> Undone, done with, soon done with, and yet
>   clearly and dangerously sweet
> Of us, the wimpled-water-dimpled, not-by-
>   morning-matchèd face,
> The flower of beauty, fleece of beauty, too too
>   apt to, ah ! to fleet,

58

Never fleets more, fastened with the tenderest
    truth
To its own best being and its loveliness of
    youth. . . .'

Than this, Hopkins truly wrote, ' I never did anything
more musical.' By his own verdict and his own
standards it is therefore the finest thing that Hopkins
did. Yet even here, where the general beauty is
undoubted, is not the music too obvious ? Is it not
always on the point of degenerating into a jingle—as
much an exhibition of the limitations of a poetical
theory as of its capabilities ? The tyranny of the
' avant toute chose ' upon a mind in which the other
things were not stubborn and self-assertive is apparent.
Hopkins's mind was irresolute concerning the quality
of his own poetical ideal. A coarse and clumsy
assonance seldom spread its snare in vain. Exquisite
openings are involved in disaster:—

  ' When will you ever, Peace, wild wood dove, shy
      wings shut,
  Your round me roaming end, and under be my
      boughs ?
  When, when, Peace, will you, Peace ? I'll not
      play hypocrite
  To own my heart: I yield you do come some-
      times; but
  That piecemeal peace is poor peace. What pure
      peace. . . .'

And the more wonderful opening of ' Windhover '
likewise sinks, far less disastrously, but still perceptibly:—

'I caught this morning morning's minion, king-
    dom of daylight's dauphin, dapple-dawn-
    drawn Falcon, in his riding
Of the rolling level underneath him steady
    air, and striding
High there, how he rung upon the rein of a
    wimpling wing
In his ecstasy! then off, off forth on swing,
As a skate's heel sweeps smooth on a bow-
    bend: the hurl and the gliding
Rebuffed the big wind. My heart in
    hiding
Stirred for a bird,—the achieve of, the mastery
    of the thing!'

We have no doubt that 'stirred for a bird' was an
added excellence to the poet's ear; to our sense it is
a serious blemish on lines which have 'the roll, the
rise, the carol, the creation.'

There is no good reason why we should give
characteristic specimens of the poet's obscurity, since
our aim is to induce people to read him. The
obscurities will slowly vanish and something of the
intention appear; and they will find in him many of
the strange beauties won by men who push on to the
borderlands of their science; they will speculate
whether the failure of his whole achievement was due
to the starvation of experience which his vocation
imposed upon him, or to a fundamental vice in his
poetical endeavour. For ourselves we believe that
the former was the true cause. His 'avant toute
chose' whirling dizzily in a spiritual vacuum, met
with no salutary resistance to modify, inform, and

strengthen it.   Hopkins told the truth of himself—
the reason why he must remain a poets' poet:—

> ' I want the one rapture of an inspiration.
>   O then if in my lagging lines you miss
>   The roll, the rise, the carol, the creation,
>   My winter world, that scarcely yields that bliss
> Now, yields you, with some sighs, our explanation.'
>
> [JUNE, 1919.

The Problem of Keats

IT is a subject for congratulation that a second edition of Sir Sidney Colvin's life of Keats[1] has been called for by the public: first, because it is a good, a very good book, and secondly, because all evidence of a general curiosity concerning a poet so great and so greatly to be loved must be counted for righteousness. The impassioned and intimate sympathy which is felt—as we may at least conclude—by a portion of the present generation for Keats is a motion of the consciousness which stands in a right and natural order. Keats is with us; and it argues much for a generous elasticity in Sir Sidney Colvin's mind, which we have neither the right nor the custom to expect in an older generation, that he should have had more than a sidelong vision of at least one aspect of the community between his poet-hero and a younger race which has had the destiny to produce far more heroes than poets. Commenting upon the inability of the late Mr Courthope to appreciate Keats, Sir Sidney writes:—

'He supposed that Keats was indifferent to history or politics. But of history he was in fact an assiduous reader, and the secret of his indifference to politics, so far as it existed, was that those of his own time had to men of his years and way of thinking been a disillusion,—that the saving of the world

---

[1] *John Keats : His Life and Poetry, His Friends, Critics, and After-fame.* By Sidney Colvin. Second edition. (Macmillan.)

62

from the grip of one great overshadowing tyranny
had but ended in reinstating a number of ancient and
minor tyrannies less interesting but not less tyrannical.
To that which lies behind and above politics and history
to the general destinies, aspirations, and tribulations
of the race, he was, as we have seen, not indifferent
but only tragically and acutely sensitive.'

We believe that both the positive and the negative of
that vindication might be exemplified among chosen
spirits to-day, living or untimely dead; but we desire,
not to enlist Sir Sidney in a cause, but only to make
apparent the reason why, in spite of minor dissents
and inevitable differences of estimation, our sympathy
with him is enduring. It may be that we have chosen
to identify ourselves so closely with Keats that we
feel to Sir Sidney the attachment that is reserved for
the staunch friend of a friend who is dead; but we
do not believe that this is so. We are rather attached
by the sense of a loyalty that exists in and for itself;
more intimate repercussions may follow, but they can
follow only when the critical honesty, the determination to let Keats be valid as Keats, whatever it might
cost (and we can see that it sometimes costs Sir Sidney
not a little), has impressed itself upon us.

It is rather by this than by Sir Sidney's particular
contributions to our knowledge of the poet that we
judge his book. This assured, we accept his patient
exposition of the theme of 'Endymion' with a friendly
interest that would certainly not be given to one with
a lesser claim upon us; and in this spirit we can also
find a welcome for the minute investigation of the
pictorial and plastic material of Keats's imagination.

63

Under auspices less benign we might have found the former mistaken and the latter irrelevant; but it so happens that when Sir Sidney shows us over the garden every goose is a swan. Like travellers who at the end of a long day's journey among an inhospitable peasantry are, against their expectation, received in a kindly farm, and find themselves talking glibly to their host of matters which are unimportant and unknown to them—the price of land, and the points of a pedigree bull—so we follow with an intense and intelligent absorption a subtle argument in ' Endymion ' in which at no moment we really believe. On the contrary, we are convinced (when we are free from our author's friendly spell) that Keats wrote ' Endymion ' at all adventure. The words of the cancelled preface : ' Before I began I had no inward feel of being able to finish; and as I proceeded my steps were all uncertain,' were, we are sure, quite literally true, and if anything an under-statement of his lack of argument and plan. Not that we believe that Keats was incapable of or averse to ' fundamental brain-work '—he had an understanding more robust, firmer in its hold of reality, more closely cast upon experience, than any one of his great contemporaries, Wordsworth not excepted—but at that phase in his evolution he was simply not concerned with understanding. ' Endymion ' is not a record or sublimation of experience; it is itself an experience. It was the liberation of a verbal inhibition, and the magic word of freedom was Beauty. The story of Endymion was to Keats a road to the unknown, in her course along which his imagination might ' paw up against the sky.'

The Problem of Keats

A refusal to admit that Keats built ' Endymion ' upon any structure of argument, however obscure— even Sir Sidney would acknowledge that the argument he discovers is *very* obscure—is so far from being a derogation from his genius that it is in our opinion necessary to a full appreciation of his idiosyncrasy. It is customary to regard the Odes as the pinnacle of his achievement and to trace a poetical progression to that point and a subsequent decline: we are shown the evidence of this decline in the revised Induction to ' Hyperion.' As far as an absolute poetical perfection is concerned there can be no serious objection to the view. But the case of Keats is eminently one to be considered in itself as well as objectively. There is no danger that Keats's poetry will not be appreciated; the danger is that Keats may not be understood. And precisely this moment is opportune for understanding him. As Mr T. S. Eliot has lately pointed out, the development of English poetry since the early nineteenth century was largely based on the achievement of two poets of genius, Keats and Shelley, who never reached maturity. They were made gods; and rightly, had not poets themselves bowed down to them. That was ridiculous; there is something even pitiful in the spectacle of Rossetti and Morris finding the culmination of poetry, the one in ' The Eve of St Agnes,' the other in ' La Belle Dame sans Merci.' And this undiscriminating submission of a century to the influence of hypostatised phases in the development of a poet of sanity and genius is perhaps the chief of the causes of the half-conscious, and for the most part far less discriminating, spirit of revolt which is at work in modern poetry.

A sense is abroad that the tradition has somehow
been snapped, that what has been accepted as the
tradition unquestioningly for a hundred years is only
a *cul de sac.* Somewhere there has been a substitution.
In the resulting chaos the twittering of bats is taken
for poetry, and the critically minded have the grim
amusement of watching verse-writers gain eminence
by imitating Coventry Patmore! The bolder spirits
declare that there never was such a thing as a tradition,
that it is no use learning, because there is nothing to
learn. But they are a little nervous for all their bold-
ness, and they prefer to hunt in packs, of which the
only condition of membership is that no one should
ask what it is.

At such a juncture, if indeed not at all times, it
is of no less importance to understand Keats than to
appreciate his poetry. The culmination of the
achievement of the Keats to be understood is not the
Odes, perfect as they are, nor the tales—a heresy
even for objective criticism—nor ' Hyperion '; but
precisely that revised Induction to ' Hyperion ' which
on the other argument is held to indicate how the
poet's powers had been ravaged by disease and the
pangs of unsatisfied love. On the technical side
alone the Induction is of extraordinary interest.
Keats's natural and proper revulsion from the Miltonic
style, the deliberate art of which he had handled like
an almost master, is evident but incomplete; he is
hampered by the knowledge that the virus is in his
blood. The creative effort of the Induction was
infinitely greater than is immediately apparent. Keats
is engaged in a war on two fronts : he is struggling
against the Miltonic manner, and struggling also to

deal with an unfamiliar content. The whole direction of his poetic purpose had shifted since he wrote ' Hyperion.' ' Hyperion,' though far finer as art, had been produced by an impulse substantially the same as ' Endymion '; it was an exercise in a manner. Keats desired to prove to himself, and perhaps a little at that moment to prove to the world, that he was capable of Miltonic discipline and grandeur. It was, most strictly, necessary for him to be inwardly certain of this. He had drunk, as deeply as any of his contemporaries, of the tradition; he needed to know that he had assimilated what he had drunk, that he could employ a conscious art as naturally as the most deliberate artist of the past, and, most of all, that he would begin, when he did begin, at the point where his forerunners left off, and not at a point behind them. These necessities were not present in this form to Keats's mind when he began ' Hyperion '; most probably he began merely with the idea of holding his own with Milton, and with a delight in an apt and congenial theme. Keats was not a poet of definite and deliberate plans, which indeed are incident to a certain tenuity of soul; his decisions were taken not by the intellect, but by the being.

He dropped ' Hyperion ' because it was inadequate to the whole of him. He was weary of its deliberate art because it interposed a veil between him and that which he needed to express; it was an imposition upon himself.

' I have given up " Hyperion "—there were too many Miltonic inversions in it—Miltonic verse cannot be written but in an artful, or rather artist's, humour.

I wish to give myself up to other sensations. English ought to be kept up. It may be interesting to you to pick out some lines from " Hyperion " and put a mark + to the false beauty proceeding from art, and one ‖ to the true voice of feeling. . . .'—(Letter to J. H. Reynolds, Sept. 22, 1819.)

That outwardly negative reaction is packed with positive implications. ' English ought to be kept up ' meant, on Keats's lips, a very great deal. But there is other and more definite authority for the positive direction in which he was turning. To his brother George he wrote, at the same time:—

' I have but lately stood on my guard against Milton. Life to him would be death to me. Miltonic verse cannot be written, but is the verse of art. I wish to devote myself to another verse alone.'

More definite still is the letter of November 17, 1819, to his friend and publisher, John Taylor:—

' I have come to a determination not to publish anything I have now ready written; but for all that to publish a poem before long and that I hope to make a fine one. As the marvellous is the most enticing and the surest guarantee of harmonious numbers I have been endeavouring to persuade myself to untether fancy and to let her manage for herself. I and myself cannot agree about this at all. Wonders are no wonders to me. I am more at home amongst Men and Women. I would rather read Chaucer than Ariosto. The little dramatic skill I may as yet have, however badly it might show in a Drama, would, I think, be sufficient for a Poem. I wish to diffuse the colouring of St Agnes Eve throughout a poem in which Character and Sentiment would be the figures to such drapery. Two or three such poems, if God should spare me, written in the course of the next six years would be a famous gradus ad Parnassum altissimum. I mean they would nerve me up to the writing of a few fine plays—my greatest ambition—when I do feel ambitious. . . .'

No letter could be saner, nor more indicative of calm resolve. Yet the precise determination is that nothing that went to make the 1820 volume should be published, neither Odes, nor Tales, nor ' Hyperion.' This is that mood of Keats which Sir Sidney Colvin, in his comment upon a passage in the revised Induction, calls one of ' fierce injustice to his own achievements and their value.' But a poet, if he is a real one, judges his own achievements not by those of his contemporaries, but by the standard of his own intention.

The evidence that Keats's mind had passed beyond the stage at which it could be satisfied by the poems of the 1820 volume is overwhelming. His letters to George of April, 1819, show that he was naturally evolving towards an attitude, a philosophy, more profound and comprehensive than could be expressed adequately in such records of momentary aspiration and emotion as the Odes; though the keen and sudden poignancy that had invaded them belongs to the new Keats. They mark the transition to the new poetry which he vaguely discerned. The problem was to find the method. The letters we have quoted to show his reaction from the Miltonic influence display the more narrowly 'artistic' aspect of the same evolution. A technique more responsive to the felt reality of experience must be found—'English ought to be kept up '—the apparatus of Romantic story must be abandoned—' Wonders are no wonders to me '—yet the Romantic colour must be kept to restore to a realistic psychology the vividness and richly various quality that are too often lost by analysis. We do not believe that we have in any respect forced the interpretation of the letters; the terminology of that age needs to be translated to be understood. ' Men and Women . . . Characters and Sentiments ' are called, for better or worse, ' psychology ' nowadays. And our translation has this merit, that some of our ultra-moderns will listen to the word ' psychology,' where they would be bat-blind to ' Characters ' and stone-deaf to ' Sentiments.'

Modern poetry is still faced with the same problem; but very few of its adepts have reached so far as to be able to formulate it even with the precision of Keats's scattered allusions. Keats himself was struck down at the moment when he was striving (against disease and against a devouring, hopeless love-passion) to face it squarely. The revised Induction reveals him in the effort to shape the traditional (and perhaps still necessary) apparatus of myth to an instrument of his attitude. The meaning of the Induction is not difficult to discover; but current criticism has the habit of regarding it dubiously. Therefore we may be forgiven for attempting, with the brevity imposed upon us, to make its elements clear. The first eighteen lines, which Sir Sidney

Colvin on objective grounds regrets are, we think, vital.

> 'Fanatics have their dreams, wherewith they
>   weave
> A paradise for a sect; the savage, too,
> From forth the loftiest fashion of his sleep
> Guesses at heaven; pity these have not
> Trac'd upon vellum or wild Indian leaf
> The shadows of melodious utterance,
> But bare of laurel they live, dream, and die;
> For poesy alone can tell her dreams,—
> With the fine spell of words alone can save
> Imagination from the sable chain
> And dumb enchantment. Who alive can say,
> 'Thou art no poet—mays't not tell thy dreams'?
> Since every man whose soul is not a clod
> Hath visions and would speak, if he had loved,
> And been well-nurtured in his mother-tongue.
> Whether the dream now purposed to rehearse
> Be poet's or fanatic's will be known
> When this warm scribe, my hand, is in the
>   grave.'

We may admit that the form of these lines is unfortunate; but we cannot wish them away. They bear most closely upon the innermost argument of the poem as Keats endeavoured to reshape it. All men, says Keats, have their visions of reality; but the poet alone can express his, and the poet himself may at the last prove to have been a fanatic, one who has imagined 'a paradise for a sect' instead of a heaven for all humanity.

This discovery marks the point of crisis in Keats's development. He is no longer content to be the singer; his poetry must be adequate to all experience. No wonder then that the whole of the new Induction centres about this thought. He describes his effort to fight against an invading death and to reach the altar in the mighty dream palace. As his foot touches the altar-step life returns, and the prophetic voice of the veiled goddess reveals to him that he has been saved by his power ' to die and live again before Thy fated hour.'

> ' " None can usurp this height," return'd that
> shade.
> " But those to whom the miseries of the world
> Are misery and will not let them rest.
> All else who find a haven in the world
> Where they may thoughtless sleep away their
> days,
> If by a chance into this fane they come,
> Rot on the pavement where thou rottedst
> half." '

Because he has been mindful of the pain in the world, the poet has been saved. But the true lovers of humanity,—

> ' Who love their fellows even to the death,
> Who feel the giant agony of the world,'

are greater than the poets; ' they are no dreamers weak.'

72

' They come not here, they have no thought to
        come,
    And thou art here for thou are less than they.'

It is a higher thing to mitigate the pain of the world
than to brood upon the problem of it. And not only
the lover of mankind, but man the animal is pre-
eminent above the poet-dreamer. His joy is joy;
his pain, pain. ' Only the dreamer venoms *all* his
days.' Yet the poet has his reward; it is given to
him to partake of the vision of the veiled Goddess—
memory, Moneta, Mnemosyne, the spirit of the
eternal reality made visible.

            ' Then saw I a wan face
    Not pined by human sorrows, but bright-
            blanch'd
    By an immortal sickness which kills not;
    It works a constant change, which happy death
    Can put no end to; deathwards progressing
    To no death was that visage; it had past
    The lily and the snow; and beyond these
    I must not think now, though I saw that face.
    But for her eyes I should have fled away;
    They held me back with a benignant light
    Soft, mitigated by divinest lids
    Half-closed, and visionless entire they seemed
    Of all external things; they saw me not,
    But in blank splendour beam'd like the mild
            moon
    Who comforts those she sees not, who knows
            not
    What eyes are upward cast. . . .'

This vision of Moneta is the culminating point of Keats's evolution. It stands at the summit, not of his poetry, but of his achievement regarded as obedient to its own inward law. Moneta was to him the discovered spirit of reality; her vision was the vision of necessity itself. In her, joy and pain, life and death, compassion and indifference, vision and blindness are one; she is the eternal abode of contraries, the Idea, if you will, not hypostatised but immanent. Before this reality the poet is impotent as his fellows; he is above them by his knowledge of it, but below them by the weakness which that knowledge brings. He, too, is the prey of contraries, the mirror of his deity, struck to the heart of his victory, enduring the intolerable pain of triumph.

Here, not unfittingly, in his struggle with a conception too big to express, came the end of Keats the poet. None have passed beyond him; few have been so far. Of the poetry that might have been constructed on the basis of an apprehension so profound we can form only a conjecture, each after his own image : we do not know the method of the 'other verse' of which Keats had a glimpse; we only know the quality with which it would have been saturated, the calm and various light of united contraries.

We fear that Sir Sidney Colvin will not agree with our view. The angles of observation are different. The angle at which we have placed ourselves is not wholly advantageous—from it Sir Sidney's book could not have been written—but it has this advantage, that from it we can read his book with a heightened interest. As we look out from it, some things are increased and some diminished with the change of perspective; and among those which are increased is our gratitude to Sir Sidney. In the clear mirror of his sympathy and sanity nothing is obscured. We are shown the Keats who wrote the perfect poems that will last with the English language, and in the few places where Sir Sidney falls short of the spirit of complete acceptance, we discern behind the words of rebuke and regret only the idealisation of a love which we are proud to share. [JULY, 1919.

Thoughts on Tchehov

WE do not know if the stories collected in this volume[1] stand together in the Russian edition of Tchehov's works, or if the selection is due to Mrs Constance Garnett. It is also possible that the juxtaposition is fortuitous. But the stories are united by a similarity of material. Whereas in the former volumes of this admirable series Tchehov is shown as preoccupied chiefly with the life of the *intelligentsia*, here he finds his subjects in priests and peasants, or (in the story *Uprooted*) in the half-educated.

Such a distinction is, indeed, irrelevant. As Tchehov presents them to our minds, the life of the country and the life of the town produce the same final impression, arouse in us an awareness of an identical quality; and thus, the distinction, by its very irrelevance, points us the more quickly to what is essential in Tchehov. It is that his attitude, to which he persuades us, is complete, not partial. His comprehension radiates from a steady centre, and is not capriciously kindled by a thousand accidental contacts. In other words, Tchehov is not what he is so often assumed to be, an impressionist. Consciously or unconsciously he had taken the step—the veritable *salto mortale*—by which the great literary artist moves out of the ranks of the minor writers. He had slowly shifted his angle of vision until he

[1] *The Bishop ; and Other Stories.* By Anton Tchehov. Translated by Constance Garnett. (Chatto & Windus.)

76

could discern a unity in multiplicity. Unity of this rare kind cannot be imposed as, for instance, Zola attempted to impose it. It is an emanation from life which can be distinguished only by the most sensitive contemplation.

The problem is to define this unity in the case of each great writer in whom it appears. To apprehend it is not so difficult. The mere sense of unity is so singular and compelling that it leaves room for few hesitations. The majority of writers, however excellent in their peculiar virtues, are not concerned with it: at one moment they represent, at another they may philosophise, but the two activities have no organic connection, and their work, if it displays any evolution at all, displays it only in the minor accidents of the craft, such as style in the narrower and technical sense, or the obvious economy of construction. There is no danger of mistaking these for great writers. Nor, in the more peculiar case of writers who attempt to impose the illusion of unity, is the danger serious. The apparatus is always visible; they cannot afford to do without the paraphernalia of argument which supplies the place of what is lacking in their presentation. The obvious instance of this legerdemain is Zola; a less obvious, and therefore more interesting example is Balzac.

To attempt the more difficult problem. What is most peculiar to Tchehov's unity is that it is far more nakedly æsthetic than that of most of the great writers before him. Other writers of a rank equal to his—and there are not so very many—have felt the need to shift their angle of vision until they could perceive an all-embracing unity; but they were not satisfied

77

with this. They felt, and obeyed, the further need of taking an attitude towards the unity they saw. They approved or disapproved, accepted or rejected it. It would be perhaps more accurate to say that they gave or refused their endorsement. They appealed to some other element than their own sense of beauty for the final verdict on their discovery; they asked whether it was just or good.

The distinguishing mark of Tchehov is that he is satisfied with the unity he discovers. Its uniqueness is sufficient for him. It does not occur to him to demand that it should be otherwise or better. The act of comprehension is accompanied by an instantaneous act of acceptance. He is like a man who contemplates a perfect work of art; but the work of creation has been his, and has consisted in the gradual adjustment of his vision until he could see the frustration of human destinies and the arbitrary infliction of pain as processes no less inevitable, natural, and beautiful than the flowering of a plant. Not that Tchehov is a greater artist than any of his great predecessors; he is merely more wholly an artist, which is a very different thing. There is in him less admixture of preoccupations that are not purely æsthetic, and probably for this reason he has less creative vigour than any other artist of equal rank. It seems as though artists, like cattle and fruit trees, need a good deal of crossing with substantial foreign elements, in order to be very vigorous and very fruitful. Tchehov has the virtues and the shortcomings of the pure case.

I do not wish to be understood as saying that Tchehov is a manifestation of *l'art pour l'art*, because in any commonly accepted sense of that phrase, he is not. Still, he might be considered as an exemplification of what the phrase might be made to mean. But instead of being diverted into a barren dispute over terminologies, one may endeavour to bring into prominence an aspect of Tchehov which has an immediate interest—his modernity. Again, the word is awkward. It suggests that he is fashionable, or up to date. Tchehov is, in fact, a good many phases in advance of all that is habitually described as modern in the art of literature. The artistic problem which he faced and solved is one that is, at most, partially present to the consciousness of the modern writer— to reconcile the greatest possible diversity of content with the greatest possible unity of æsthetic impression. Diversity of content we are beginning to find in profusion—Miss May Sinclair's latest experiment shows how this need is beginning to trouble a writer with a settled manner and a fixed reputation—but how rarely do we see even a glimmering recognition of the necessity of a unified æsthetic impression! The modern method is to assume that all that is, or has been, present to consciousness is *ipso facto* unified æsthetically. The result of such an assumption is an obvious disintegration both of language and artistic effort, a mere retrogression from the classical method.

The classical method consisted, essentially, in achieving æsthetic unity by a process of rigorous exclusion of all that was not germane to an arbitrary (because non-æsthetic) argument. This argument was let down like a string into the saturated solution of the consciousness until a unified crystalline structure congregated about it. Of all great artists of the past Shakespeare is the richest in his departures from this

79

method. How much deliberate artistic purpose there was in his employment of songs and madmen and fools (an employment fundamentally different from that made by his contemporaries) is a subject far too big for a parenthesis. But he, too, is at bottom a classic artist. The modern problem—it has not yet been sufficiently solved for us to speak of a modern method—arises from a sense that the classical method produces over-simplification. It does not permit of a sufficient sense of multiplicity. One can think of a dozen semi-treatments of the problem from Balzac to Dostoevsky, but they were all on the old lines. They might be called Shakespearean modifications of the classical method.

Tchehov, we believe, attempted a treatment radically new. To make use again of our former image in his maturer writing, he chose a different string to let down into the saturated solution of consciousness. In a sense he began at the other end. He had decided on the quality of æsthetic impression he wished to produce, not by an arbitrary decision, but by one which followed naturally from the contemplative unity of life which he had achieved. The essential quality he discerned and desired to represent was his argument, his string. Everything that heightened and completed this quality accumulated about it, quite independently of whether it would have been repelled by the old criterion of plot and argument. There is a magnificent example of his method in the longest story in this volume, 'The Steppe.' The quality is dominant throughout, and by some strange compulsion it makes heterogeneous things one; it is reinforced by the incident. Tiny events—the

peasant who eats minnows alive, the Jewish innkeeper's brother who burned his six thousand roubles
—take on a character of portent, except that the word
is too harsh for so delicate a distortion of normal
vision; rather it is a sense of incalculability that haunts
us. The emphases have all been slightly shifted,
but shifted according to a valid scheme. It is not
while we are reading, but afterwards that we wonder
how so much significance could attach to a little
boy's questions in a remote village shop:—

‘ “ How much are these cakes ? ’
‘ “ Two for a farthing.’
‘ Yegorushka took out of his pocket the cake
given him the day before by the Jewess and asked
him:—
‘ “ And how much do you charge for cakes like
this ? ’
‘ The shopman took the cake in his hands, looked
at it from all sides, and raised one eyebrow.
‘ “ Like that ? ’ he asked.
‘ Then he raised the other eyebrow, thought a
minute, and answered:—
‘ “ Two for three farthings. . . .” ’

It is foolish to quote it. It is like a golden pebble
from the bed of a stream. The stream that flows
over Tchehov's innumerable pebbles, infinitely diverse
and heterogeneous, is the stream of a deliberately
sublimated quality. The figure is inexact, as figures
are. Not every pebble could be thus transmuted.
But how they are chosen, what is the real nature of
the relation which unites them, as we feel it does, is

a secret which modern English writers need to explore. Till they have explored and mastered it Tchehov will remain a master in advance of them.   [AUGUST, 1919.

THE case of Tchehov is one to be investigated again and again because he is the only great modern artist in prose.   Tolstoy was living throughout Tchehov's life, as Hardy has lived throughout our own, and these are great among the greatest.   But they are not modern.   It is an essential part of their greatness that they could not be; they have a simplicity and scope that manifestly belongs to all time rather than to this.   Tchehov looked towards Tolstoy as we to Hardy.   He saw in him a Colossus, one whose achievement was of another and a greater kind than his own.

' I am afraid of Tolstoy's death.   If he were to die there would be a big empty place in my life.   To begin with, because I have never loved any man as much as him. . . . Secondly, while Tolstoy is in literature it is easy and pleasant to be a literary man; even recognising that one has done nothing and never will do anything is not so dreadful, since Tolstoy will do enough for all.   His work is the justification of the enthusiasms and expectations built upon literature.   Thirdly, Tolstoy takes a firm stand; he has an immense authority, and so long as he is alive, bad tastes in literature, vulgarity of every kind, insolent and lachrymose, all the bristling, exasperated vanities will be in the far background, in the shade. . . .'— (January, 1900.)

Tchehov was aware of the gulf that separated him from the great men before him, and he knew that it yawned so deep that it could not be crossed. He belonged to a new generation, and he alone perhaps was fully conscious of it. 'We are lemonade,' he wrote in 1892.

'Tell me honestly who of my contemporaries— that is, men between thirty and forty-five—have given the world one single drop of alcohol? . . . Science and technical knowledge are passing through a great period now, but for our sort it is a flabby, stale, dull time. . . . The causes of this are not to be found in our stupidity, our lack of talent, or our insolence, but in a disease which for the artist is worse than syphilis or sexual exhaustion. We lack "something," that is true, and that means that, lift the robe of our muse, and you will find within an empty void. Let me remind you that the writers who we say are for all time or are simply good, and who intoxicate us, have one common and very important characteristic: they are going towards something and are summoning you towards it, too, and you feel, not with your mind but with your whole being, that they have some object, just like the ghost of Hamlet's father, who did not come and disturb the imagination for nothing. . . . And we? We! We paint life as it is, but beyond that—nothing at all. . . . Flog us and we can do more! We have neither immediate nor remote aims, and in our soul there is a great empty space. We have no politics, we do not believe in revolution, we have no God, we are not afraid of ghosts, and I personally am not afraid even of death and blindness.

One who wants nothing, hopes for nothing, and fears nothing cannot be an artist. . . .

'. . . You think I am clever. Yes, I am at least so far clever as not to conceal from myself my disease and not to deceive myself, and not to cover up my own emptiness with other people's rags, such as the ideas of the 'sixties and so on.'

That was written in 1892. When we remember all the strange literary effort gathered round about that year in the West—Symbolism, the *Yellow Book*, Art for Art's sake—and the limbo into which it has been thrust by now, we may realise how great a precursor, and, in his own despite, a leader, Anton Tchehov was. When Western literature was plunging with enthusiasm into one *cul de sac* after another, incapable of diagnosing its own disease, Tchehov in Russia, unknown to the West, had achieved a clear vision and a sense of perspective.

To-day we begin to feel how intimately Tchehov belongs to us; to-morrow we may feel how infinitely he is still in advance of us. A genius will always be in advance of a talent, and in so far as we are concerned with the genius of Tchehov we must accept the inevitable. We must analyse and seek to understand it; we must, above all, make up our minds that since Tchehov has written and his writings have been made accessible to us, a vast amount of our modern literary production is simply unpardonable. Writers who would be modern and ignore Tchehov's achievement are, however much they may persuade themselves that they are devoted artists, merely engaged in satisfying their vanity or in the exercise of a profession like

84

any other; for Tchehov is a standard by which modern literary effort must be measured, and the writer of prose or poetry who is not sufficiently single-minded to apply the standard to himself is of no particular account.

Though Tchehov's genius is, strictly speaking, inimitable, it deserves a much exacter study than it has yet received. The publication of this volume of his letters[1] hardly affords the occasion for that; but it does afford an opportunity for the examination of some of the chief constituents of his perfect art. These touch us nearly because—we insist again—the supreme interest of Tchehov is that he is the only great modern artist in prose. He belongs, as we have said, to us. If he is great, then he is great not least in virtue of qualities which we may aspire to possess; if he is an ideal, he is an ideal to which we can refer ourselves. He had been saturated in all the disillusions which we regard as peculiarly our own, and every quality which is distinctive of the epoch of consciousness in which we are living now is reflected in him—and yet, miracle of miracles, he was a great artist. He did not rub his cheeks to produce a spurious colour of health; he did not profess beliefs which he could not maintain; he did not seek a reputation for universal wisdom, or indulge himself in self-gratifying dreams of a millennium which he alone had the ability to control. He was and wanted to be nothing in particular, and yet, as we read these letters of his, we feel gradually form within ourselves the conviction that he was a hero—more than that, *the* hero of our time.

It is significant that, in reading Tchehov's letters,

[1] *Letters of Anton Tchehov.* Translated by Constance Garnett (Chatto & Windus).

we do not consider him under the aspect of an artist. We are inevitably fascinated by his character as a man, one who, by efforts which we have most frequently to divine for ourselves from his reticences, worked on the infinitely complex material of the modern mind and soul, and made it in himself a definite, positive, and most lovable thing. He did not throw in his hand in face of his manifold bewilderments; he did not fly for refuge to institutions in which he did not believe; he risked everything, in Russia, by having no particular faith in revolution and saying so. In every conjuncture of his life that we can trace in his letters he behaved squarely by himself, and, since he is our great exemplar, by us. He refused to march under any political banner—a thing, let it be remembered, of almost inconceivable courage in his country; he submitted to savagely hostile attacks for his political indifference; yet he spent more of his life and energy in doing active good to his neighbour than all the high-souled professors of liberalism and social reform. He undertook an almost superhuman journey to Sahalin in 1890 to investigate the condition of the prisoners there; in 1892 he spent the best part of a year as a doctor devising preventive measures against the cholera in the country district where he lived, and, although he had no time for the writing on which his living depended, he refused the government pay in order to preserve his own independence of action; in another year he was the leading spirit in organising practical measures of famine relief about Nizhni-Novgorod. From his childhood to his death, moreover, he was the sole support of his family. Measured by the standards of Christian morality, Tchehov was wholly a saint. His self-devotion was boundless.

Yet we know he was speaking nothing less than the truth of himself when he wrote: ' It is essential to be indifferent.' Tchehov was indifferent; but his indifference, as a mere catalogue of his secret philanthropies will show, was of a curious kind. He made of it, as it were, an axiomatic basis of his own self-discipline. Since life is what it is and men are what they are, he seems to have argued, everything depends upon the individual. The stars are hostile, but love is kind, and love is within the compass of any man if he will work to attain it. In one of his earliest letters he defines true culture for the benefit of his brother Nikolay, who lacked it. Cultivated persons, he said, respect human personality; they have sympathy not for beggars and cats only; they respect the property of others, and therefore pay their debts; they are sincere and dread lying like fire; they do not disparage themselves to arouse compassion; they have no shallow vanity; if they have a talent they respect it; they develop the æsthetic feeling in themselves . . . they seek as far as possible to restrain and ennoble the sexual instinct. The letter from which these chief points are taken is tremulous with sympathy and wit. Tchehov was twenty-six when he wrote it. He concludes with the words: ' What is needed is constant work day and night, constant reading, study, will. Every hour is precious for it.'

In that letter are given all the elements of Tchehov the man. He set himself to achieve a new humanity, and he achieved it. The indifference upon

which Tchehov's humanity was built was not therefore a moral indifference; it was, in the main, the
recognition and acceptance of the fact that life itself
is indifferent. To that he held fast to the end. But
the conclusion which he drew from it was not that it
made no particular difference what any one did, but
that the attitude and character of the individual were
all-important. There was, indeed, no panacea, political
or religious, for the ills of humanity; but there could
be a mitigation in men's souls. But the new asceticism
must not be negative. It must not cast away the
goods of civilisation because civilisation is largely a
sham.

' Alas! I shall never be a Tolstoyan. In women I
love beauty above all things, and in the history of
mankind, culture expressed in carpets, carriages with
springs, and keenness of wit. Ach! To make haste
and become an old man and sit at a big table!'

Not that there is a trace of the hedonist in
Tchehov, who voluntarily endured every imaginable
hardship if he thought he could be of service to his
fellow-men, but, as he wrote elsewhere, ' we are
concerned with pluses alone.' Since life is what it is,
its amenities are doubly precious. Only they must
be amenities without humbug.

' Pharisaism, stupidity, and despotism reign not
in bourgeois houses and prisons alone. I see them in
science, in literature, in the younger generation.
. . . That is why I have no preference either for
gendarmes, or for butchers, or for scientists, or for
88

writers, or for the younger generation. I regard
trade marks and labels as a superstition. My holy
of holies is the human body, health, intelligence,
talent, inspiration, love, and the most absolute freedom
—freedom from violence and lying, whatever forms
they make take. This is the programme I would
follow if I were a great artist.'

What 'the most absolute freedom' meant to Tchehov
his whole life is witness. It was a liberty of a purely
moral kind, a liberty, that is, achieved at the cost of
a great effort in self-discipline and self-refinement.
In one letter he says he is going to write a story about
the son of a serf—Tchehov was the son of a serf—who
'squeezed the slave out of himself.' Whether the
story was ever written we do not know, but the process
is one to which Tchehov applied himself all his life
long. He waged a war of extermination against the
lie in the soul in himself, and by necessary implication
in others also.

He was, thus, in all things a humanist. He faced
the universe, but he did not deny his own soul.
There could be for him no antagonism between
science and literature, or science and humanity. They
were all pluses; it was men who quarrelled among
themselves. If men would only develop a little more
loving-kindness, things would be better. The first
duty of the artist was to be a decent man.

' Solidarity among young writers is impossible and
unnecessary. . . . We cannot feel and think in the
same way, our aims are different, or we have no aims
whatever, we know each other little or not at all, and

so there is nothing on to which this solidarity could be securely hooked. . . . And is there any need for it ? No, in order to help a colleague, to respect his personality and work, to refrain from gossiping about him, envying him, telling him lies and being hypocritical, one does not need so much to be a young writer as simply a man. . . . Let us be ordinary people, let us treat everybody alike, and then we shall not need any artificially worked-up solidarity.'

It seems a simple discipline, this moral and intellectual honesty of Tchehov's, yet in these days of conceit and coterie his letters strike us as more than strange. One predominant impression remains: it is that of Tchehov's candour of soul. Somehow he has achieved with open eyes the mystery of pureness of heart; and in that, though we dare not analyse it further, lies the secret of his greatness as a writer and of his present importance to ourselves.

[MARCH, 1920.

American Poetry

WE are not yet immune from the weakness of looking
into the back pages to see what the other men have
said; and on this occasion we received a salutary
shock from the critic of the *Detroit News*, who informs
us that Mr Aiken, ' despite the fact that he is one
of the youngest and the newest, having made his
debut less than four years ago, . . . demonstrates
. . . that he is eminently capable of taking a solo
part with Edgar Lee Masters, Amy Lowell, James
Oppenheim, Vachel Lindsay, and Edwin Arlington
Robinson.' The shock is two-fold. In a single
sentence we are in danger of being convicted of
ignorance, and, where we can claim a little knowledge,
we plead guilty; we know nothing of either Mr
Oppenheim or Mr Robinson. This very ignorance
makes us cautious where we have a little knowledge
We know something of Mr Lindsay, something of
Mr Masters, and a good deal of Miss Lowell, who
has long been a familiar figure in our anthologies of
revolt; and we cannot understand on what principle
they are assembled together. Miss Lowell is, we
·are persuaded, a negligible poet, with a tenuous and
commonplace impulse to write which she teases out
into stupid ' originalities.' Of the other two gentlemen we have seen nothing which convinces us that
they are poets, but also nothing which convinces us
that they may not be.

Moreover, we can understand how Mr Aiken
might be classed with them. All three have in common

what we may call creative energy. They are all facile, all obviously eager to say something, though it is not at all obvious what they desire to say, all with an instinctive conviction that whatever it is it cannot be said in the old ways. Not one of them produces the certainty that this conviction is really justified, or that he has tested it; not one has written lines which have the doom 'thus and not otherwise' engraved upon their substance; not one has proved that he is capable of addressing himself to the central problem of poetry, no matter what technique be employed—how to achieve a concentrated unity of æsthetic impression. They are all diffuse; they seem to be content to lead a hundred indecisive attacks upon reality at once rather than to persevere and carry a single one to a final issue; they are all multiple, careless, and slipshod—and they are all interesting.

They are extremely interesting. For one thing, they have all achieved what is, from whatever angle one looks at it, a very remarkable success. Very few people, initiate or profane, can have opened Mr Lindsay's 'Congo' or Mr Masters's 'Spoon River Anthology' or Mr Aiken's 'Jig of Forslin' without being impelled to read on to the end. That does not very often happen with readers of a book which professes to be poetry save in the case of the thronging admirers of Miss Ella Wheeler Wilcox, and their similars. There is, however, another case more exactly in point, namely, that of Mr Kipling. With Mr Kipling our three American poets have much in common, though the community must not be unduly pressed. Their most obvious similarity is the prominence into which

they throw the novel interest in their verse. They
are, or at moments they seem to be, primarily tellers
of stories. We will not dogmatise and say that the
attempt is illegitimate; we prefer to insist that to
tell a story in poetry and keep it poetry is a herculean
task. It would indeed be doubly rash to dogmatise,
for our three poets desire to tell very different stories,
and we are by no means sure that the emotional
subtleties which Mr Aiken in particular aims at
capturing are capable of being exactly expressed in
prose.

Since Mr Aiken is the *corpus vile* before us we
will henceforward confine ourselves to him, though
we premise that in spite of his very sufficient originality
he is characteristic of what is most worth attention in
modern American poetry. Proceeding then, we find
another point of contact between him and Mr Kipling,
more important perhaps than the former, and certainly
more dangerous. Both find it apparently impossible
to stem the uprush of rhetoric. Perhaps they do not
try to; but we will be charitable—after all, there is
enough good in either of them to justify charity—
and assume that the willingness of the spirit gives
way to the weakness of the flesh. Of course we all
know about Mr Kipling's rhetoric; it is a kind of
emanation of the spatial immensities with which he
deals—Empires, the Seven Seas, from Dublin to
Diarbekir. Mr Aiken has taken quite another province
for his own; he is an introspective psychologist.
But like Mr Kipling he prefers big business. His
inward eye roves over immensities at least as vast as
Mr Kipling's outward. In 'The Charnel Rose and
Other Poems' this appetite for the illimitable inane of

introspection seems to have gained upon him. There
is much writing of this kind:—

> ' Dusk, withdrawing to a single lamplight
> At the end of an infinite street—
> He saw his ghost walk down that street for ever,
> And heard the eternal rhythm of his feet.
> And if he should reach at last that final gutter,
> To-day, or to-morrow,
> Or, maybe, after the death of himself and time;
> And stand at the ultimate curbstone by the stars,
> Above dead matches, and smears of paper, and
>   slime;
> Would the secret of his desire
> Blossom out of the dark with a burst of fire ?
> Or would he hear the eternal arc-lamps sputter,
> Only that; and see old shadows crawl;
> And find the stars were street lamps after all ?
>
> Music, quivering to a point of silence,
> Drew his heart down over the edge of the
>   world. . . .'

It is dangerous for a poet to conjure up infinities
unless he has made adequate preparation for keeping
them in control when they appear. We are afraid
that Mr Aiken is almost a slave of the spirits he has
evoked. Dostoevsky's devil wore a shabby frock-
coat, and was probably managing-clerk to a solicitor at
twenty-five shillings a week. Mr Aiken's incubus is,
unfortunately, devoid of definition; he is protean and
unsatisfactory.

' I am confused in webs and knots of scarlet
Spun from the darkness;
Or shuttled from the mouths of thirsty spiders.

Madness for red!   I devour the leaves of
    autumn.
I tire of the green of the world.
I am myself a mouth for blood. . . .'

Perhaps we do wrong to ask ourselves whether this
and similar things mean, exactly, anything ?   Mr
Aiken warns us that his intention has been to use the
idea—'the impulse which sends us from one dream
or ideal to another, always disillusioned, always
creating for adoration some new and subtler fiction '
—' as a theme upon which one might wilfully build
a kind of absolute music.'   But having given us so
much instruction, he should have given more; he
should have told us in what province of music he has
been working.   Are we to look for a music of verbal
melody, or for a musical elaboration of an intellectual
theme ?   We infer, partly from the assurance that
' the analogy to a musical symphony is close,' more
from the absence of verbal melody, that we are to
expect the elaboration of a theme.   In that case the
fact that we have a more definite grasp of the theme
in the programme-introduction than anywhere in the
poem itself points to failure.   In the poem ' stars rush
up and whirl and set,' ' skeletons whizz before and
whistle behind,' ' sands bubble and roses shoot soft
fire,' and we wonder what all the commotion is about.
When there is a lull in the pandemonium we have a
glimpse, not of eternity, but precisely of 1890:—

> ' And he saw red roses drop apart,
> Each to disclose a charnel heart. . . .

We are far from saying that Mr Aiken's poetry is merely a chemical compound of the 'nineties, Freud, and introspective Imperialism; but we do think it is liable to resolve at the most inopportune moments into those elements, and that such moments occur with distressing frequency in the poem called ' The Charnel Rose.' ' Senlin ' resists disruption longer. But the same elements are there. They are better but not sufficiently fused. The rhetoric forbids, for there is no cohesion in rhetoric. We have the sense that Mr Aiken felt himself inadequate to his own idea, and that he tried to drown the voice of his own doubt by a violent clashing of the cymbals where a quiet recitative was what the theme demanded and his art could not ensure.

> ' Death himself in the rain . . . death him-
>   self . . .
> Death in the savage sunlight . . . skeletal
>   death . . .
> I hear the clack of his feet,
> Clearly on stones, softly in dust,
> Speeding among the trees with whistling
>   breath,
> Whirling the leaves, tossing his hands from
>   waves . . .
> Listen! the immortal footsteps beat and
>   beat! . . .'

We are persuaded that Mr Aiken did not mean to say

that; he wanted to say something much subtler. But to find exactly what he wanted might have taken him many months. He could not wait. Up rushed the rhetoric; bang went the cymbals: another page, another book. And we, who have seen great promise in his gifts, are left to collect some inadequate fragments where his original design is not wholly lost amid the poor expedients of the moment. For Mr Aiken never pauses to discriminate. He feels that he needs rhyme; but any rhyme will do:—

> ' Has no one, in a great autumnal forest,
> When the wind bares the trees with mournful
>   tone,
> Heard the sad horn of Senlin slowly blown ? '

So he descends to a poetaster's padding. He does not stop to consider whether his rhyme interferes with the necessary rhythm of his verse; or, if he does, he is in too much of a hurry to care, for the interference occurs again and again. And these disturbances and deviations, rhetoric and the sacrifice of rhythm to shoddy rhyme, appear more often than the thematic outline itself emerges.

In short, Mr Aiken is, at present, a poet whom we have to take on trust. We never feel that he meant exactly what he puts before us, and, on the whole, the evidence that he meant something better, finer, more irrevocably itself, is pretty strong. We catch in his hurried verses at the swiftly passing premonition of a *frisson* hitherto unknown to us in poetry, and as we recognise it, we recognise also the great distance he has to travel along the road of art, and the great labour that he must perform before he becomes something more than a brilliant feuilletonist in verse. It is hardly for us to prophesy whether he will devote the labour. His fluency tells us of his energy, but tells us nothing of its quality. We can only express our hope that he will, and our conviction that if he were to do so his great pains, and our lesser ones would be well requited.

[SEPTEMBER, 1919.

Ronsard

RONSARD is *rangé* now; but he has not been in that
position for so very long, a considerably shorter
time, for instance, than any one of the Elizabethans
(excepting Shakespeare) with us. Sainte-Beuve was
very tentative about him until the sixties, when his
dubious, half-patronising air made way for a safe
enthusiasm. And, even now, it can hardly be said
that French critical opinion about him has crystallised;
the late George Wyndham's essay shows a more
convinced and better documented appreciation than
any that we have read in French, based as it is on the
instinctive sympathy which one landed gentleman
who dabbles in the arts feels towards another who
devotes himself to them—an admiration which does
not exclude familiarity.

Indeed, it is precisely because Ronsard lends
himself so superbly as an amateur to treatment by
the amateur, that any attempt to approach him more
closely seems to be tinged with rancour or ingratitude.
There is something churlish in the determination to
be most on one's guard against the engaging graces
of the amateur, a sense that one is behaving like the
hero of a Gissing novel; but the choice is not large.
One must regard Ronsard either as a charming
country gentleman, or as a great historical figure in
the development of French poetry, or as a poet; and
the third aspect has a chance of being the most
important.

Ronsard is pre-eminently the poet of a simple

99

mind. There is nothing mysterious about him or his poetry; there is not even a perceptible thread of development in either. They are equable, constant, imperturbable, like the bag of a much invited gun, or the innings of a safe batsman. The accomplishment is akin to an animal endowment. The nerves, instead of being, if only for a moment, tense and agitated, are steady to a degree that can produce an exasperation in a less well-appointed spectator. He will never let himself down, or give himself away, one feels, until the admiration of an apparent sure restraint passes into the conviction that there is nothing to restrain. All Ronsard the poet is in his poetry, and indeed on the surface of it.

Poetry was not therefore, as one is tempted to think sometimes, for Ronsard a game. There was plenty of game in it; *l'art de bien Pétrarquiser* was all he claimed for himself. But the game would have wearied any one who was not aware that he could be completely satisfied and expressed by it. Ronsard was never weary. However much one may tire of him, the fatigue never is infected by the nausea which is produced by some of the mechanical sonnet sequences of his contemporaries. No one reading Ronsard ever felt the tedium of mere nullity. It would be hard to find in the whole of M. van Bever's exhaustive edition of 'Les Amours'[1] a single piece which has not its sufficient charge of gusto. When you are tired, it is because you have had enough of that particular kind of man and mind; you know him too well, and can reckon too closely the chances of a shock of surprise.

[1] *Les Amours.* Par Pierre de Ronsard. Texte établi par Ad. van Bever. Two volumes. (Paris: Crès.)

With the more obvious, and in their way delightful, surprises Ronsard is generous. He can hold the attention longer than any poet of an equal tenuity of matter. Chiefly for two reasons, of which one is hardly capable of further analysis. It is the obvious reality of his own delight in 'Petrarchising.' He is perpetually in love with making; he disports himself with a childlike enthusiasm in his art. There are moments when he seems hardly to have passed beyond the stage of naïve wonder that words exist and are manipulable.

> ' Dous fut le trait, qu'Amour hors de sa trousse
> Pour me tuer, me tira doucement,
> Quand je fus pris au dous commencement
> D'une douceur si doucettement douce. . . .'

Ronsard is here a boy playing knucklebones with language; and some of his characteristic excellences are little more than a development of this aptitude, with its more striking incongruities abated. A modern ear can be intoxicated by the charming jingle of

> ' Petite Nimfe folastre,
> Nimfette que j'idolastre. . . .'

One does not pause to think how incredibly naïve it is compared with Villon, who had not a fraction of Ronsard's scholarship, or even with Clément Marot; naïve both in thought and art. As for the stature of the artist, we are back with Charles of Orleans. It would be idle to speculate what exactly Villon would have made of the atomic theory had he read Lucretius;

but we are certain that he would have done something very different from Ronsard's

> ' Les petits cors, culbutant de travers,
>   Parmi leur cheute en biais vagabonde,
>   Heurtés ensemble ont composé le monde,
>   S'entr'acrochant d'acrochemens divers. . . .'

For this is not grown-up; the cut to simplicity has been too short. So many of Ronsard's verses flow over the mind, without disturbing it; fall charmingly on the ear, and leave no echoes. But for the moment we share his enjoyment.

The second cause of his continued power of attraction is doubtless allied to the first; it is a *naïveté* of a particular kind, which differs from the profound ingenuousness of which we have spoken by the fact that it is employed deliberately. Conscious simplicity is art, and if it is successful art of no mean order. Ronsard's method of admitting us, as it were, to his conversation with himself is definitely his own. His interruptions of a verse with ' Hà ' or ' Hé'; his ' Mon Dieu, que j'aime! ' or ' Hé, que ne suis-je puce ? ' (the difference between Ronsard's flea and Donne's would be worth examination) have in them an element of irresistible *bonhomie*. We feel that he is making us his confidant. He does not have to tear agonies out of himself, so that what he confides has no chance of making explicit any secrets of our own. There is nothing dangerous about him; we know that he is as safe as we are. We are in conversation, not communion. But how effective and engaging it is!

' Vous ne le voulez pas ?   Eh bien, je suis
        contant . . .'

' Hé, Dieu du ciel, je n'eusse pas pensé
   Qu'un seul départ eust causé tant de peine! . . .'

or the still more casual

' Un joïeus deplaisir qui douteus l'épointelle,
   Quoi l'épointelle! ainçois le genne et le
        martelle . . .'

Of this device of style our own Elizabethans were to
make more profitable use than Ronsard.   At their
best they packed an intensity of dramatic significance
into conversational language, of which Ronsard had
no inkling; and even a strict contemporary of his,
like Wyatt, could touch cords more intimate by the
same means.   But, on the other hand, Ronsard never
fails of his own effect, which is not to convince us
emotionally, but to compel us to listen.   His unexpected address to himself or to us is a new ornament
for us to admire, not a new method for him to express
a new thing; and the suggestion of new rhythms
that might thus be attained is never fully worked
out.

' Mais tu ne seras plus ?   Et puis ? . . . quand
        la paleur
   Qui blemist nôtre corps sans chaleur ne lumière
   Nous perd le sentiment ? . . .

The ampleness of that reverberance is almost isolated.

Ronsard's resources are indeed few. But he needed few. His simple mind was at ease in a machinery of commonplaces, and he makes the pleasant impression of one to whom commonplaces are real. He felt them all over again. One imagines him reading the classics—the Iliad in three days, or his beloved companion ' sous le bois amoureux,' Tibullus —with an unfailing delight in all the concatenations of phrase which are foisted on to unripe youth nowadays in the pages of a Gradus. One might almost say that he saw his loves at second-hand, through alien eyes, were it not that he faced them with some directness as physical beings, and that the artificiality implied in the criticism is incongruous with the honesty of such a natural man. But apart from a few particulars that would find a place in a census paper one would be hard put to it to distinguish Cassandre from Hélène. What charming things Ronsard has to say of either might be said of any charming woman —' le mignard embonpoint de ce sein,'—

' Petit nombril, que mon penser adore,
    Non pas mon œil, qui n'eut oncques ce bien . . .'

And though he assures Hélène that she has turned him from his grave early style, ' qui pour chanter si bas n'est point ordonné,' the difference is too hard to detect; one is forced to conclude that it is precisely the difference between a court lady and an innkeeper's daughter. As far as art is concerned the most definite and distinctive thing that Ronsard had to say of any of his ladies is said of one to whom he put forward none of his usually engrossing pretensions.

It was the complexion of Marguerite of Navarre of which he wrote:—

> ' De vif cinabre estoit faicte sa joue,
>   Pareille au teint d'un rougissant œillet,
>   Ou d'une fraize, alors que dans de laict
>   Dessus le hault de la cresme se joue.'

That is, whether it belonged to Marguerite or not, a divine complexion. It is the kind of thing that cannot be said about two ladies; the image is too precise to be interchangeable. This may be a reason why it was applied to a lady *hors concours* for Ronsard.

But we need, in fact, seek no reason other than the circumscription of Ronsard's poetical gifts. They reduce to only two—the gift of convinced commonplace, and the gift of simple melody. His commonplace is genuine commonplace, quite distinct from the tense and pregnant condensation of a lifetime of impassioned experience in Dante or Shakespeare; things that would occur to a bookish country gentleman in after-dinner conversation, the sentiments that such a rare and amiable person would underscore in his Horace. (From a not unimportant angle Ronsard is a minor Horace.) These things are the warp of his poetry; they range from the familiar ' Le temps s'en va ' to the masterly straightforwardness of

> ' plus heureus celui qui la fera
>   Et femme et mère, en lieu d'une pucelle.'

His melody, likewise, is genuine melody; it is irrepressible. It led him to belie his own professed seriousness. He could not stop his sonnets from rippling even when he pretended to passionate argument. Life came easily to him; he was never weary of it, at the most he acknowledged that he was ' saoûl de la vie.' It is not surprising, therefore, that his remonstrances as the tortured lover have a trick of opening to a delightful tune:—

> ' Rens-moi mon cœur, rens-moi mon cœur pillarde. . . .'

In another form this melody more closely recalls Thomas Campion:—

> ' Seule je l'ai veue, aussi je meurs pour elle. . . .'

But to compare Ronsard's sonnet with ' Follow your saint ' is to see how infinitely more subtle a master of lyrical music was the Elizabethan than the great French lyrist of the Renaissance. From first to last Ronsard was an amateur. [SEPTEMBER, 1919.

Samuel Butler

THE appearance of a new impression of *The Way of all Flesh* [1] in Mr Fifield's edition of Samuel Butler's works gives us an occasion to consider more calmly the merits and the failings of that entertaining story. Like all unique works of authors who stand, even to the most obvious apprehension, aside from the general path, it has been overwhelmed with superlatives. The case is familiar enough and the explanation is simple and brutal. It is hardly worth while to give it. The truth is that although there is no inherent reason why the isolated novel of an author who devotes himself to other forms should not be 'one of the great novels of the world,' the probabilities tell heavily against it. On the other hand, an isolated novel makes a good stick to beat the age. It is fairly certain to have something sufficiently unique about it to be useful for the purpose. Even its blemishes have a knack of being *sui generis*. To elevate it is, therefore, bound to imply the diminution of its contemporaries.

Yet, apart from the general argument, there are particular reasons why the praise of *The Way of all Flesh* should be circumspect. Samuel Butler knew extraordinarily well what he was about. His novel was written intermittently between 1872 and 1884 when he abandoned it. In the twenty remaining years of his life he did nothing to it, and we have Mr

---

[1] *The Way of all Flesh.* By Samuel Butler. 11th impression of 2nd edition. (Fifield.)

Streatfeild's word for it that 'he professed himself dissatisfied with it as a whole, and always intended to rewrite, or at any rate, to revise it.' We could have deduced as much from his refusal to publish the book. The certainty of commercial failure never deterred Butler from publication; he was in the happy situation of being able to publish at his own expense a book of whose merit he was himself satisfied. His only reason for abandoning *The Way of all Flesh* was his own dissatisfaction with it. His instruction that it should be published in its present form after his death proves nothing against his own estimate. Butler knew, at least as well as we, that the good things in his book were legion. He did not wish the world or his own reputation to lose the benefit of them.

But there are differences between a novel which contains innumerable good things and a great novel. The most important is that a great novel does not contain innumerable good things. You may not pick out the plums, because the pudding falls to pieces if you do. In *The Way of all Flesh*, however, a *compère* is always present whose business it is to say good things. His perpetual flow of asides is pleasant because the asides are piquant and, in their way, to the point. Butler's mind, being a good mind, had a predilection for the object, and his detestation of the rotunder platitudes of a Greek chorus, if nothing else, had taught him that a corner-man should have something to say on the subject in hand. His arguments are designed to assist his narrative; moreover, they are sympathetic to the modern mind. An enlightened hedonism is about all that is left to us, and Butler's hatred of humbug is, though a little more placid, like our own. We share his ethical likes and dislikes. As an audience we are ready to laugh at his asides, and, on the first night at least, to laugh at them even when they interrupt the play.

But our liking for the theses cannot alter the fact that *The Way of all Flesh* is a *roman à thèses*. Not that there is anything wrong with the *roman à thèses*, if the theses emerge from the narrative without its having to be obviously doctored. Nor does it matter very much that a *compère* should be present all the while, provided that he does not take upon himself to replace the demonstration the narrative must afford, by arguments outside it. But what happens in *The Way of all Flesh*? We may leave aside the minor thesis of heredity, for it emerges, gently enough, from the story; besides, we are not quite sure what it is. We have no doubt, on the other hand, about the major thesis; it is blazoned on the title page, with its sub-malicious quotation from St Paul to the Romans. ' We know that all things work together for good to them that love God.' The necessary gloss on this text is given in Chapter LXVIII, where Ernest, after his arrest, is thus described:—

' He had nothing more to lose; money, friends, character, all were gone for a very long time, if not for ever; but there was something else also that had taken its flight along with these. I mean the fear of that which man could do unto him. *Cantabit vacuus.* Who could hurt him more than he had been hurt already? Let him but be able to earn his bread, and he knew of nothing which he dared not venture if it would make the world a happier place for those who were young and lovable. Herein he found so much comfort that he almost wished he had lost his reputation even more completely—for he saw that it was like a man's life which may be found of them that lose it and lost of them that would find it. He should not have had the courage to give up all for Christ's sake, but now Christ had mercifully taken all, and lo! it seemed as though all were found.

' As the days went slowly by he came to see that Christianity and the denial of Christianity after all met as much as any other extremes do; it was a fight about names—not about things; practically the Church of Rome, the Church of England, and the freethinker have the same ideal standard and meet in the gentleman; for he is the most perfect saint who is the most perfect gentleman. . . .'

With this help the text and the thesis can be translated : ' All experience does a gentleman good.' It is the kind of thing we should like very much to believe; as an article of faith it was held with passion and vehemence by Dostoevsky, though the connotation of the word ' gentleman ' was for him very different from the connotation it had for Butler. (Butler's gentleman, it should be said in passing, was very much the ideal of a period, and not at all *quod semper*, *quod ubique* ; a very Victorian anti-Victorianism.) Dostoevsky worked his thesis out with a ruthless devotion to realistic probability. He emptied the cornucopia of misery upon his heroes and drove them to suicide one after another; and then had the audacity to challenge the world to say that they were not better, more human, and more lovable for the disaster in which they were inevitably overwhelmed. And, though it is hard to say ' Yes ' to his challenge, it is harder still to say ' No.'

In the case of Ernest Pontifex, however, we do not care to respond to the challenge at all. The experiment is faked and proves nothing. It is mere humbug to declare that a man has been thrown into the waters of life to sink or swim, when there is an anxious but cool-headed friend on the bank with a £70,000 life-belt to throw after him the moment his head goes under. That is neither danger nor experience. Even if Ernest Pontifex knew nothing of the future awaiting him (as we are assured he did not) it makes no difference. *We* know he cannot sink; he is a lay figure with a pneumatic body. Whether he became a lay figure for Butler also we cannot say; we can merely register the fact that the book breaks down after Ernest's misadventure with Miss Maitland, a deplorably unsubstantial episode to be the crisis of a piece of writing so firm in texture and solid in values as the preceding chapters. Ernest as a man has an intense non-existence.

After all, as far as the positive side of *The Way of all Flesh*' is concerned, Butler's eggs are all in one basket. If the adult Ernest does not materialise, the book hangs in empty air. Whatever it may be instead it is not a great novel, nor even a good one. So much established, we may begin to collect the good things. Christina is the best of them. She is, by any standard, a remarkable creation. Butler was ' all round ' Christina. Both by analysis and synthesis she is wholly his. He can produce her in either way. She lives as flesh and blood and has not a little of our affection; she is also constructed by definition, ' If it were not too awful a thing to say of anybody, she meant well '—the whole phrase gives exactly Christina's stature. Alethea Pontifex is really a bluff; but the bluff succeeds, largely because, having experience of Christina, we dare not call it. Mrs Jupp is triumphantly complete; there are even moments when she seems as great as Mrs Quickly. The novels that contain three such women (or two if we reckon the uncertain Alethea, who is really only a vehicle for Butler's very best sayings, as cancelled by the non-existent Ellen) can be counted, we suppose, on our ten fingers.

Of the men, Theobald is well worked out (in both senses of the word). But we know little of what went on inside him. We can fill out Christina with her inimitable day-dreams; Theobald remains something of a skeleton, whereas we have no difficulty at all with Dr Skinner, of Roughborough. We have a sense of him in retirement steadily filling the shelves with volumes of Skinner, and we know how it was done. When he reappears we assume the continuity of his existence without demur. The glimpse of George Pontifex is also satisfying; after the christening party we know him for a solid reality. Pryer was half-created when his name was chosen. Butler did the rest in a single paragraph which contains a perfect delineation of ' the Oxford manner ' twenty years before it had become a disease known to ordinary diagnosis. The curious may find this towards the beginning of Chapter LI. But Ernest, upon whom so much depends, is a phantom—a dream-child waiting the incarnation which Butler refused him for twenty years. Was it laziness, was it a felt incapacity ? We do not know; but in the case of a novelist it is our duty to believe the worst. The particularity of our attitude to Butler appears in the fact that we are disappointed, not with him, but with Ernest. We are even angry with that young man. If it had not been for him, we believe, *The Way of all Flesh* might have appeared in 1882; it might have short-circuited *Robert Elsmere.*   [JUNE, 1919.

WE approach the biography of an author whom we respect, and therefore have thought about, with contradictory feelings. We are excited at the thought of finding our conclusions reinforced, and apprehensive less the compact and definite figure which our imaginations have gradually shaped should become vague and incoherent and dull. It is a pity to purchase enlightenment at the cost of definition; and it is more important that we should have a clear notion of the final shape of a man in whom we are interested than an exact record of his phases.

The essential quality of great artists is incommensurable with biography; they seem to be unconsciously engaged in a perpetual evasion of the event. All that piety can do for them is beside the mark. Their wilful spirit is fled before the last stone of the mausoleum can be got in place, and as it flies it jogs the elbow of the cup-bearer and his libation is spilt idly upon the ground. Although it would be too much and too ungrateful to say that the monumental piety of Mr Festing Jones has been similarly turned

to derision—after all, Butler was not a great man—
we feel that something analogous has happened.
This laborious building is a great deal too large for
him to dwell in. He had made himself a cosy habitation in the *Note-Books*, with the fire in the right place
and fairly impervious to the direct draughts of
criticism. In a two-volume memoir[1] he shivers
perceptibly, and at moments he looks faintly ridiculous,
more than faintly pathetic.

And if it be said that a biography should make no
difference to our estimate of the man who lives and
has his being in his published works, we reply that
it shifts the emphasis. An amusingly wrong-headed
book about Homer is a peccadillo; ten years of life
lavished upon it is something a good deal more serious.
And even *The Way of all Flesh*, which as an experi-
mental novel is a very considerable achievement,
becomes something different when we have to regard
it as a laborious and infinitely careful record of
experienced fact. Further still, even the edge of
the perfected inconsequence of certain of the ' Notes '
is somewhat dulled when we see the trick of it being
exercised. The origin of the amusing remark on
Blake, who ' was no good because he learnt Italian
at over 60 in order to read Dante, and we know
Dante was no good because he was so fond of Virgil,
and Virgil was no good because Tennyson ran him
—well, Tennyson goes without saying,' is to be
found in ' No, I don't like Lamb. You see, Canon
Ainger writes about him, and Canon Ainger goes to
tea with my aunts.' Repeated, it becomes merely a

[1] *Samuel Butler, author of ' Erewhon '* (1835-1902) : *a Memoir.* By
Henry Festing Jones. 2 vols. (Macmillan.)

clever way of being stupid, as we should be if we were tempted to say we couldn't bear Handel, because Butler was mad on him, and Butler was no good because he was run by Mr Jones, and, well, Mr Jones goes without saying.

Nevertheless, though Butler lives with much discomfort and some danger in Mr Jones's tabernacle, he does continue to live. What his head loses by the inquisition of a biography his heart gains, though we wonder whether Butler himself would have smiled upon the exchange. Butler loses almost the last vestige of a title to be considered a creative artist when the incredible fact is revealed that the letters of Theobald and Christina in *The Way of all Flesh* are merely reproduced from those which his father and mother sent him. Nor was Butler, even as a copyist, always adequate to his originals. The brilliantly witty letters of Miss Savage, by which the first volume is made precious, seem to us to indicate a real woman upon whom something more substantial might have been modelled than the delightful but evanescent picture of Alethea Pontifex. Here, at least, is a picture of Miss Savage and Butler together which, to our sense, gives some common element in both which escaped the expression of the author of *The Way of all Flesh*:—

' I like the cherry-eating scene, too [Miss Savage wrote after reading the MS. of *Alps and Sanctuaries*], because it reminded me of your eating cherries when I first knew you. One day when I was going to the gallery, a very hot day I remember, I met you on the shady side of Berners Street, eating cherries out

115

of a basket. Like your Italian friends, you were perfectly silent with content, and you handed the basket to me as I was passing, without saying a word. I pulled out a handful and went on my way rejoicing, without saying a word either. I had not before perceived you to be different from any one else. I was like Peter Bell and the primrose with the yellow brim. As I went away to France a day or two after that and did not see you again for months, the recollection of you as you were eating cherries in Berners Street abode with me and pleased me greatly.'

Again, we feel that the unsubstantial Towneley of the novel should have been more like flesh and blood when we learn that he too was drawn from the life, and from a life which was intimately connected with Butler's. Here, most evidently, the heart gains what the head loses, for the story of Butler's long-suffering generosity to Charles Paine Pauli is almost beyond belief and comprehension. Butler had met Pauli, who was two years his junior, in New Zealand, and had conceived a passionate admiration for him. Learning that he desired to read for the bar, Butler, who had made an unexpected success of his sheep-farming, offered to lend him £100 to get to England and £200 a year until he was called. Very shortly after they both arrived in England, Pauli separated from Butler, refusing even to let him know his address, and thenceforward paid him one brief visit every day. He continued, however, to draw his allowance regularly until his death all through the period when, owing to the failure of Butler's investments, £200 seems to have been a good deal more than one-half Butler's income. At Pauli's death in 1897 Butler discovered what he must surely at moments have suspected, that Pauli had been making between £500 and £800 at the bar, and had left about £9000—not to Butler. Butler wrote an account of the affair after Pauli's death which is strangely self-revealing:—

'. . . Everything that he had was good, and he was such a fine handsome fellow, with such an attractive manner that to me he seemed everything I should like myself to be, but knew very well that I was not. . . .

' I had felt from the very beginning that my intimacy with Pauli was only superficial, and I also perceived more and more that I bored him. . . . He liked society and I hated it. Moreover, he was at times very irritable and would find continual fault with me; often, I have no doubt, justly, but often, as it seemed to me, unreasonably. Devoted to him as I continued to be for many years, those years were very unhappy as well as very happy ones.

' I set down a great deal to his ill-health, no doubt truly; a great deal more, I was sure, was my own fault—and I am so still; I excused much on the score of his poverty and his dependence on myself—for his father and mother, when it came to the point, could do nothing for him; I was his host and was bound to forbear on that ground if on no other. I always hoped that, as time went on, and he saw how absolutely devoted to him I was, and what unbounded confidence I had in him, and how I forgave him over and over again for treatment which I would not have stood for a moment from any one else—I always hoped that he would soften and deal as frankly and unreservedly with me as I with him; but, though for some fifteen years I hoped this, in the end I gave it up, and settled down into a resolve from which I never departed—to do all I could for him, to avoid friction of every kind, and to make the best of things for him and myself that circumstances would allow.'

In love such as this there is a feminine tenderness and devotion which positively illuminates what otherwise appears to be a streak of perversity in Butler; and the illumination becomes still more certain when we read Butler's letters to the young Swiss, Hans Faesch, to whom *Out into the Night* was written. Faesch had departed for Singapore.

' The sooner we all of us,' wrote Butler, ' as men of sense and sober reason, get through the very acute, poignant sorrow which we now feel, the better for us all. There is no fear of any of us forgetting when the acute stage is passed. I should be ashamed of myself ·for having felt as keenly and spoken with as little reserve as I have if it were any one but you; but I feel no shame at any length to which grief can take me when it is about you. I can call to mind no word which ever passed between us three which had been better unspoken: no syllable of irritation or unkindness; nothing but goodness and kindness ever came out of you, and such as our best was we gave it to you as you gave yours to us. Who may not well be plunged up to the lips in sorrow at parting from one of whom he can say this in all soberness

and truth ?   I feel as though I had lost an only son
with no hope of another. . . .'

The love is almost pathetically lavish.   Letters like
these reveal to us a man so avid of affection that he
must of necessity erect every barrier and defence to
avoid a mortal wound.   His sensibility was *rentrée*,
probably as a consequence of his appalling childhood;
and the indication helps us to understand not only
the inordinate suspiciousness with which he behaved
to Darwin, but the extent to which irony was his
favoured weapon.   The most threatening danger for
such a man is to take the professions of the world at
their face value; he can inoculate himself only by
irony.   The more extreme his case, the more devouring
the hunger to love and be loved, the more extreme
the irony, and in Butler it reached the absolute
maximum, which is to interpret the professions of
the world as their exact opposite.   As a reviewer
of the *Note-Books* in *The Athenæum* recently said,
Butler's method was to stand propositions on their
heads.   He universalised his method; he applied it
not merely to scientific propositions of fact, but, even
more ruthlessly, to the converse of daily life.   He
divided up the world into a vast majority who meant
the opposite of what they said, and an infinitesimal
minority who were sincere.   The truth that the vast
majority are borderland cases escaped him, largely
because he was compelled by his isolation to regard
all his honest beliefs as proven certainties.   That a
man could like and admire him and yet regard him
as in many things mistaken and wrong-headed was
strictly incomprehensible to him, and from this angle

the curious relations which existed between him and Dr Richard Garnett of the British Museum are of uncommon interest. They afford a strange example of mutual mystification.

Thus at least one-half the world, not of life only (which does not greatly matter, for one can live as happily with half the world as with the whole) but of thought, was closed to him. Most of the poetry, the music, and the art of the world was humbug to him, and it was only by insisting that Homer and Shakespeare were exactly like himself that he managed to except them from his natural aversion. So, in the last resort, he humbugged himself quite as vehemently as he imagined the majority of men were engaged in humbugging him. If his standard of truth was higher than that of the many, it was lower than that of the few. There is a kingdom where the crass division into sheep and goats is merely clumsy and inopportune. In the slow meanderings of this *Memoir* we too often catch a glimpse of Butler measuring giants with the impertinent foot-rule of his common sense. One does not like him the less for it, but it is, in spite of all the disconcerting jokes with which it may be covered, a futile and ridiculous occupation. Persistently there emerges from the record the impression of something childish, whether in petulance or *gaminerie*, a crudeness as well as a shrewdness of judgment and ideal. Where Butler thought himself complete, he was insufficient; and where he thought himself insufficient, he was complete. To himself he appeared a hobbledehoy by the side of Pauli; to us he appears a hobbledehoy by the side of Miss Savage.

[OCTOBER, 1919.

The Poetry of Mr Hardy

ONE meets fairly often with the critical opinion that Mr Hardy's poetry is incidental. It is admitted on all sides that his poetry has curious merits of its own, but it is held to be completely subordinate to his novels, and those who maintain that it must be considered as having equal standing with his prose, are not seldom treated as guilty of paradox and preciousness.

We are inclined to wonder, as we review the situation, whether those of the contrary persuasion are not allowing themselves to be impressed primarily by mere bulk, and arguing that a man's chief work must necessarily be what he has done most of; and we feel that some such supposition is necessary to explain what appears to us as a visible reluctance to allow Mr Hardy's poetry a clean impact upon the critical consciousness. It is true that we have ranged against us critics of distinction, such as Mr Lascelles Abercrombie and Mr Robert Lynd, and that it may savour of impertinence to suggest that the case could have been unconsciously pre-judged in their minds when they addressed themselves to Mr Hardy's poetry. Nevertheless, we find some significance in the fact that both these critics are of such an age that when they came to years of discretion the Wessex Novels were in existence as a *corpus*. There, before their eyes, was a monument of literary work having a unity unlike that of any contemporary author. The poems became public only after they had laid the foundations of their judgment. For them Mr Hardy's work was done. Whatever he might subsequently produce was an interesting, but to their criticism an otiose appendix to his prose achievement.

It happens therefore that to a somewhat younger critic the perspective may be different. By the accident of years it would appear to him that Mr Hardy's poetry was no less a *corpus* than his prose. They would be extended equally and at the same moment before his eyes; he would embark upon voyages of discovery into both at roughly the same time; and he might find, in total innocence of preciousness and paradox, that the poetry would yield up to him a quality of perfume not less essential than any that he could extract from the prose.

This is, as we see it, the case with ourselves. We discover all that our elders discover in Mr Hardy's novels; we see more than they in his poetry. To our mind it exists superbly in its own right; it is not lifted into significance upon the glorious substructure of the novels. They also are complete in themselves. We recognise the relation between the achievements, and discern that they are the work of a single mind; but they are separate works, having separate and unique excellences. The one is only approximately explicable in terms of the other. We incline, therefore, to attach a signal importance to what has always seemed to us the most important sentence in *Who's Who ?*—namely, that in which Mr Hardy confesses that in 1868 he was compelled—that is his own word —to give up writing poetry for prose.

For Mr Hardy's poetic gift is not a late and freakish flowering. In the volume into which has been gathered

122

all his poetical work with the exception of ' The Dynasts,'[1] are pieces bearing the date 1866 which display an astonishing mastery, not merely of technique but of the essential content of great poetry. Nor are such pieces exceptional. Granted that Mr Hardy has retained only the finest of his early poetry, still there are a dozen poems of 1866-7 which belong either entirely or in part to the category of major poetry. Take, for instance, ' Neutral Tones ':—

' We stood by a pond that winter day,
  And the sun was white, as though chidden of
    God,
  And a few leaves lay on the starving sod;
    —They had fallen from an ash, and were
    gray.

' Your eyes on me were as eyes that rove
  Over tedious riddles long ago;
  And some winds played between us to and fro
  On which lost the more by our love.

' The smile on your mouth was the deadest thing
  Alive enough to have strength to die;
  And a grin of bitterness swept thereby
  Like an ominous bird a-wing. . . .

' Since then keen lessons that love deceives
  And wrings with wrong, have shaped to me
  Your face, and the God-curst sun, and a tree
  And a pond edged with grayish leaves.'

[1] *Collected Poems of Thomas Hardy.* Vol. I. (Macmillan.)

That was written in 1867. The date of *Desperate Remedies*, Mr Hardy's first novel, was 1871. *Desperate Remedies* may have been written some years before. It makes no difference to the astonishing contrast between the immaturity of the novel and the maturity of the poem. It is surely impossible in the face of such a juxtaposition then to deny that Mr Hardy's poetry exists in its own individual right, and not as a curious simulacrum of his prose.

These early poems have other points of deep interest, of which one of the chief is in a sense technical. One can trace a quite definite influence of Shakespeare's sonnets in his language and imagery. The four sonnets, ' She to Him ' (1866), are full of echoes, as :—

> ' Numb as a vane that cankers on its point
> True to the wind that kissed ere canker came.'

or this from another sonnet of the same year :—

> ' As common chests encasing wares of price
> Are borne with tenderness through halls of
> state.'

Yet no one reading the sonnets of these years can fail to mark the impress of an individual personality. The effect is, at times, curious and impressive in the extreme. We almost feel that Mr Hardy is bringing some physical compulsion to bear on Shakespeare and forcing him to say something that he does not want to say. Of course, it is merely a curious tweak of the fancy; but there comes to us in such lines as the following an insistent vision of two youths of an

124

age, the one masterful, the other indulgent, and carrying out his companion's firm suggestion:—

> ' Remembering mine the loss is, not the blame
> That Sportsman Time rears but his brood to
>   kill,
> Knowing me in my soul the very same—
> One who would die to spare you touch of ill!—
> Will you not grant to old affection's claim
> The hand of friendship down Life's sunless hill?'

But, fancies aside, the effect of these early poems is twofold. Their attitude is definite:—

> ' Crass Casualty obstructs the sun and rain
> And dicing time for gladness calls a moan . . .
> These purblind Doomsters had as readily
>   thrown
> Blisses about my pilgrimage as pain.'

and the technique has the mark of mastery, a complete economy of statement which produces the conviction that the words are saying only what poet ordained they should say, neither less nor more.

The early years were followed by the long period of the novels, in which, we are prepared to admit, poetry was actually if not in intention incidental. It is the grim truth that poetry cannot be written in between times; and, though we have hardly any dates on which to rely, we are willing to believe that few of Mr Hardy's characteristic poems were written between the appearance of *Desperate Remedies* and his farewell to the activity of novel-writing with *The Well-Beloved* (1897). But the few dates which we have tell us that ' Thoughts of Phena,' the beautiful poem beginning:—

> ' Not a line of her writing have I,
> Not a thread of her hair. . . .'

which reaches forward to the love poems of 1912-13, was written in 1890.

Whether the development of Mr Hardy's poetry was concealed or visible during the period of the novels, development there was into a maturity so overwhelming that by its touchstone the poetical work of his famous contemporaries appears singularly jejune and false. But, though by the accident of social conditions—for that Mr Hardy waited till 1898 to publish his first volume of poems is more a social than an artistic fact—it is impossible to follow out the phases of his poetical progress in the detail we would desire, it is impossible not to recognise that the mature poet, Mr Hardy, is of the same poetical substance as the young poet of the 'sixties. The attitude is unchanged; the modifications of the theme of ' crass casualty ' leave its central asseveration unchanged. There are restatements, enlargements of perspective, a slow and forceful expansion of the personal into the universal, but the truth once recognised is never suffered for a moment to be hidden or mollified. Only a superficial logic would point, for instance, to his

> ' Wonder if Man's consciousness
> Was a mistake of God's,'

as a denial of ' casualty.' To envisage an accepted truth from a new angle, to turn it over and over again in the mind in the hope of finding some aspect which might accord with a large and general view is the inevitable movement of any mind that is alive and not dead. To say that Mr Hardy has finally discovered unity may be paradoxical; but it is true. The harmony of the artist is not as the harmony of the preacher or the philosopher. Neither would grant, neither would understand the profound acquiescence that lies behind 'Adonais' or the 'Ode to the Grecian Urn.' Such acquiescence has no moral quality, as morality is even now understood, nor any logical compulsion. It does not stifle anger nor deny anguish; it turns no smiling face upon unsmiling things; it is not puffed up with the resonance of futile heroics. It accepts the things that are as the necessary basis of artistic creation. This unity which comes of the instinctive refusal in the great poet to deny experience, and subdues the self into the whole as part of that which is not denied, is to be found in every corner of Mr Hardy's mature poetry. It gives, as it alone can really give, to personal emotion what is called the impersonality of great poetry. We feel it as a sense of background, a conviction that a given poem is not the record, but the culmination of an experience, and that the experience of which it is the culmination is far larger and more profound than the one which it seems to record.

At the basis of great poetry lies an all-embracing realism, an adequacy to all experience, a refusal of the merely personal in exultation or dismay. Take the contrast between Rupert Brooke's deservedly famous lines: 'There is some corner of a foreign field . . .' and Mr Hardy's 'Drummer Hodge':—

> ' Yet portion of that unknown plain
>   Will Hodge for ever be;
>   His homely Northern heart and brain
>   Grow to some Southern tree,
>   And strange-eyed constellations reign
>   His stars eternally.'

We know which is the truer. Which is the more beautiful ? Is it not Mr Hardy ? And which (strange question) is the more consoling, the more satisfying, the more acceptable ? Is it not Mr Hardy ? There is sorrow, but it is the sorrow of the spheres. And this, not the apparent anger and dismay of a self's discomfiture, is the quality of greatness in Mr Hardy's poetry. The Mr Hardy of the love poems of 1912-13 is not a man giving way to memory in poetry; he is a great poet uttering the cry of the universe. A vast range of acknowledged experience returns to weight each syllable; it is the quality of life that is vocal, gathered into a moment of time with a vista of years :—

> ' Ignorant of what there is flitting here to see,
>   The waked birds preen and the seals flop
>   lazily,
>   Soon you will have, Dear, to vanish from me,
>   For the stars close their shutters and the
>   Dawn whitens hazily.
>   Trust me, I mind not, though Life lours
>   The bringing me here; nay, bring me here
>   again!
>   I am just the same as when
>   Our days were a joy and our paths through
>   flowers.'
>   [NOVEMBER, 1919.

The Poetry of Mr Hardy

WE have read these poems of Thomas Hardy, read them not once, but many times. Many of them have already become part of our being; their indelible impress has given shape to dumb and striving elements in our soul; they have set free and purged mute, heart-devouring regrets. And yet, though this is so, the reading of them in a single volume, the submission to their movement with a like unbroken motion of the mind, gathers their greatness, their poignancy and passion, into one stream, submerging us and leaving us patient and purified.

There have been many poets among us in the last fifty years, poets of sure talent, and it may be even of genius, but no other of them has this compulsive power. The secret is not hard to find. Not one of them is adequate to what we know and have suffered. We have in our own hearts a new touchstone of poetic greatness. We have learned too much to be wholly responsive to less than an adamantine honesty of soul and a complete acknowledgment of experience. 'Give us the whole,' we cry, 'give us the truth.' Unless we can catch the undertone of this acknowledgment, a poet's voice is in our ears hardly more than sounding brass or a tinkling cymbal.

Therefore we turn—some by instinct and some by deliberate choice—to the greatest; therefore we deliberately set Mr Hardy among these. What they have, he has, and has in their degree—a plenary vision of life. He is the master of the fundamental theme; it enters into, echoes in, modulates and modifies all his particular emotions, and the individual poems of which they are the substance. Each work of his is a fragment of a whole—not a detached and arbitrarily severed fragment, but a unity which implies, calls for and in a profound sense creates a vaster and completely comprehensive whole. His reaction to an episode has behind and within it a reaction to the universe. An overwhelming endorsement descends upon his words: he traces them as with a pencil, and straightway they are graven in stone.

Thus his short poems have a weight and validity which sets them apart in kind from even the very finest work of his contemporaries. These may be perfect in and for themselves; but a short poem by Mr Hardy is often perfect in a higher sense. As the lines of a diagram may be produced in imagination to contain within themselves all space, one of Mr Hardy's most characteristic poems may expand and embrace all human experience. In it we may hear the sombre, ruthless rhythm of life itself—the dominant theme that gives individuation to the ripple of fragmentary joys and sorrows. Take ' The Broken Appointment ':—

> ' You did not come,
> And marching Time drew on, and wore me
>   numb.—
> Yet less for loss of your dear presence there
> Than that I thus found lacking in your
>   make
> That high compassion which can overbear
> Reluctance for pure lovingkindness' sake
> Grieved I, when, as the hope-hour stroked its
>   sum,
>   You did not come.

'You love not me,
And love alone can lend you loyalty
—I know and knew it. But, unto the store
Of human deeds divine in all but name,
Was it not worth a little hour or more
To add yet this: Once you, a woman, came
To soothe a time-torn man; even though it be
        You love not me?'

On such a seeming fragment of personal experience
lies the visible endorsement of the universe. The
hopes not of a lover but of humanity are crushed
beneath its rhythm. The ruthlessness of the event is
intensified in the motion of the poem till one can
hear the even pad of destiny; and a moment comes
when to a sense made eager by the strain of intense
attention it seems to have been written by the destiny
it records.

What is the secret of poetic power like this? We
do not look for it in technique, though the technique
of this poem is masterly. But the technique of ' as
the hope-hour stroked its sum ' is of such a kind
that we know as we read that it proceeds from a
sheer compulsive force. For a moment it startles;
a moment more and the echo of those very words
is reverberant with accumulated purpose. They are
pitiless as the poem; the sign of an ultimate obedience
is upon them. Whence came the power that compelled it? Can the source be defined or indicated?
We believe it can be indicated, though not defined.
We can show where to look for the mystery, that in
spite of our regard remains a mystery still. We are
persuaded that almost on the instant that it was felt

the original emotion of the poem was endorsed. Perhaps it came to the poet as the pain of a particular and personal experience; but in a little or a long while —creative time is not measured by days or years— it became, for him, a part of the texture of the general life. It became a manifestation of life, almost, nay wholly, in the sacramental sense, a veritable epiphany. The manifold and inexhaustible quality of life was focused into a single revelation. A critic's words do not lend themselves to the necessary precision. We should need to write with exactly the same power as Mr Hardy when he wrote ' the hope-hour stroked its sum,' to make our meaning likewise inevitable. The word ' revelation ' is fertile in false suggestion; the creative act of power which we seek to elucidate is an act of plenary apprehension, by which one manifestation, one form of life, one experience is seen in its rigorous relation to all other and to all possible manifestations, forms, and experiences. It is, we believe, the act which Mr Hardy himself has tried to formulate in the phrase which is the title of one of his books of poems—*Moments of Vision*.

Only those who do not read Mr Hardy could make the mistake of supposing that on his lips such a phrase had a mystical implication. Between belief and logic lies a third kingdom, which the mystics and the philosophers alike are too eager to forget—the kingdom of art, no less the residence of truth than the two other realms, and to some, perhaps, more authentic even than they. Therefore when we expand the word ' vision ' in the phrase to ' æsthetic vision ' we mean, not the perception of beauty, at least in the ordinary sense of that ill-used word, but the

132

apprehension of truth, the recognition of a complete system of valid relations incapable of logical statement. Such are the acts of unique apprehension which Mr Hardy, we believe, implied by his title. In a ' moment of vision ' the poet recognises in a single separate incident of life, life's essential quality. The uniqueness of the whole, the infinite multiplicity and variety of its elements, are manifested and apprehended in a part. Since we are here at work on the confines of intelligible statement, it is better, even at the cost of brutalising a poem, to choose an example from the book that bears the mysterious name. The verses that follow come from ' Near Lanivet, 1872.' We choose them as an example of Mr Hardy's method at less than its best, at a point at which the scaffolding of his process is just visible.

' There was a stunted hand-post just on the crest,
　　Only a few feet high:
She was tired, and we stopped in the twilight-
　　　　time for her rest,
　　At the crossways close thereby.

' She leant back, being so weary, against its stem,
　　And laid her arms on its own,
Each open palm stretched out to each end of
　　　　them,
　　Her sad face sideways thrown.

' Her white-clothed form at this dim-lit cease of day
　　Made her look as one crucified
In my gaze at her from the midst of the dusty way,
　　And hurriedly " Don't," I cried.

' I do not think she heard.   Loosing thence she
        said,
    As she stepped forth ready to go,
" I am rested now.—Something strange came
        into my head;
    I wish I had not leant so ! ' . . .

' And we dragged on and on, while we seemed
        to see
    In the running of Time's far glass
Her crucified, as she had wondered if she might
        be
    Some day.—Alas, alas! '

Superstition and symbolism, some may say; but
they mistakenly invert the order of the creative
process.   The poet's act of apprehension is wholly
different from the lover's fear; and of this apprehension
the chance-shaped crucifix is the symbol and not the
cause.   The concentration of life's vicissitude upon
that white-clothed form was first recognised by a
sovereign act of æsthetic understanding or intuition;
the seeming crucifix supplied a scaffolding for its
expression; it afforded a clue to the method of transposition into words which might convey the truth
thus apprehended; it suggested an equivalence.   The
distinction may appear to be hair-drawn, but we
believe that it is vital to the theory of poetry as a
whole, and to an understanding of Mr Hardy's poetry
in particular.   Indeed, in it must be sought the
meaning of another of his titles, ' Satires of Circumstance,' where the particular circumstance is neither
typical nor fortuitous, but a symbol necessary to

communicate to others the sense of a quality in life more largely and variously apprehended by the poet.

At the risk of appearing fantastic we will endeavour still further to elucidate our meaning. The poetic process is, we believe, twofold. The one part, the discovery of the symbol, the establishment of an equivalence, is what we may call poetic method. It is concerned with the transposition and communication of emotion, no matter what the emotion may be, for to poetic method the emotional material is, strictly, indifferent. The other part is an æsthetic apprehension of significance, the recognition of the all in the one. This is a specifically poetic act, or rather the supreme poetic act. Yet it may be absent from poetry. For there is no necessary connection between poetic apprehension and poetic method. Poetic method frequently exists without poetic apprehension; and there is no reason to suppose that the reverse is not also true, for the recognition of greatness in poetry is probably not the peculiar privilege of great poets. We have here, at least a principle of division between major and minor poetry.

Mr Hardy is a major poet; and we are impelled to seek further and ask what it is that enables such a poet to perform this sovereign act of apprehension and to recognise the quality of the all in the quality of the one. We believe that the answer is simple. The great poet knows what he is looking for. Once more we speak too precisely, and so falsely, being compelled to use the language of the kingdom of logic to describe what is being done in the kingdom of art. The poet, we say, knows the quality for which he seeks; but this knowledge is rather a condition than a possession of soul. It is a state of responsiveness rather than a knowledge of that to which he will respond. But it is knowledge inasmuch as the choice of that to which he will respond is determined by the condition of his soul. On the purity of that condition depends his greatness as a poet, and that purity in its turn depends upon his denying no element of his profound experience. If he denies or forgets, the synthesis—again the word is a metaphor—which must establish itself within him is fragmentary and false. The new event can wake but partial echoes in his soul or none at all; it can neither be received into, nor can it create a complete relation, and so it passes incommensurable from limbo into forgetfulness.

Mr Hardy stands high above all other modern poets by the deliberate purity of his responsiveness. The contagion of the world's slow stain has not touched him; from the first he held aloof from the general conspiracy to forget in which not only those who are professional optimists take a part. Therefore his simplest words have a vehemence and strangeness of their own:—

> ' It will have been:
> Nor God nor Demon can undo the done,
> Unsight the seen
> Make muted music be as unbegun
> Though things terrene
> Groan in their bondage till oblivion supervene.'

What neither God nor Demon can do, men are incessantly at work to accomplish. Life itself rewards

136

them for their assiduity, for she scatters her roses chiefly on the paths of those who forget her thorns. But the great poet remembers both rose and thorn; and it is beyond his power to remember them otherwise than together.

It was fitting, then, and to some senses inevitable, that Mr Hardy should have crowned his work as a poet in his old age by a series of love poems that are unique for power and passion in even the English language. This late and wonderful flowering has no tinge of miracle; it has sprung straight from the main stem of Mr Hardy's poetic growth. Into ' Veteris Vestigia Flammæ ' is distilled the quintessence of the power that created the Wessex Novels and ' The Dynasts '; all that Mr Hardy has to tell us of life, the whole of the truth that he has apprehended, is in these poems, and no poet since poetry began has apprehended or told us more. *Sunt lacrimæ rerum.* [NOVEMBER, 1919.

POSTSCRIPT

Three months after this essay was written the first volume of the long awaited definitive edition of Mr Hardy's works (the Mellstock Edition) appeared. It was with no common thrill that we read in the precious pages of introduction the following words confirming the theory upon which the first part of the essay is largely based.

' Turning now to my verse—to myself the more individual part of my literary fruitage—I would say

137

that, unlike some of the fiction, nothing interfered with the writer's freedom in respect of its form or content. Several of the poems—indeed many—were produced before novel-writing had been thought of as a pursuit; but few saw the light till all the novels had been published. . . .

'The few volumes filled by the verse cover a producing period of some eighteen years first and last, while the seventeen or more volumes of novels represent correspondingly about four-and-twenty years. One is reminded by this disproportion in time and result how much more concise and quint-essential expression becomes when given in rhythmic form than when shaped in the language of prose.'

Present Condition of English Poetry

SHALL we, or shall we not, be serious? To be serious nowadays is to be ill-mannered, and what, murmurs the cynic, does it matter? We have our opinion; we know that there is a good deal of good poetry in the Georgian book, a little in *Wheels*.[1] We know that there is much bad poetry in the Georgian book, and less in *Wheels*. We know that there is one poem in *Wheels* beside the intense and sombre imagination of which even the good poetry of the Georgian book pales for a moment. We think we know more than this. What does it matter? Pick out the good things, and let the rest go.

And yet, somehow, this question of modern English poetry has become important for us, as important as the war, important in the same way as the war. We can even analogise. *Georgian Poetry* is like the Coalition Government; *Wheels* is like the Radical opposition. Out of the one there issues an indefinable odour of complacent sanctity, an unctuous redolence of *union sacrée*; out of the other, some acidulation of perversity. In the coalition poets we find the larger number of good men, and the larger number of bad ones; in the opposition poets we find no bad ones with the coalition badness, no good ones with the coalition goodness, but in a single case a touch of the apocalyptic, intransigent, passionate

---

[1] *Georgian Poetry*, 1918-1919. Edited by E. M. (The Poetry Bookshop.)
Wheels. Fourth Cycle. (Oxford: B. H. Blackwell.)

honesty that is the mark of the martyr of art or life.

On both sides we have the corporate and the individual flavour; on both sides we have those individuals-by-courtesy whose flavour is almost wholly corporate; on both sides the corporate flavour is one that we find intensely disagreeable. In the coalition we find it noxious, in the opposition no worse than irritating. No doubt this is because we recognise a tendency to take the coalition seriously, while the opposition is held to be ridiculous. But both the coalition and the opposition—we use both terms in their corporate sense—are unmistakably the product of the present age. In that sense they are truly representative and complementary each to the other; they are a fair sample of the goodness and badness of the literary epoch in which we live; they are still more remarkable as an index of the complete confusion of æsthetic values that prevails to-day.

The corporate flavour of the coalition is a false simplicity. Of the nineteen poets who compose it there are certain individuals whom we except absolutely from this condemnation, Mr de la Mare, Mr Davies, and Mr Lawrence; there are others who are more or less exempt from it, Mr Abercrombie, Mr Sassoon, Mrs Shove, and Mr Nichols; and among the rest there are varying degrees of saturation. This false simplicity can be quite subtle. It is compounded of worship of trees and birds and contemporary poets in about equal proportions; it is sicklied over at times with a quite perceptible varnish of modernity, and at other times with what looks to be technical skill, but generally proves to be a fairly clumsy

reminiscence of somebody else's technical skill. The
negative qualities of this *simplesse* are, however, the
most obvious; the poems imbued with it are devoid
of any emotional significance whatever. If they have
an idea it leaves you with the queer feeling that it is
not an idea at all, that it has been defaced, worn
smooth by the rippling of innumerable minds. Then,
spread in a luminous haze over these compounded
elements, is a fundamental right-mindedness; you
feel, somehow, that they might have been very
wicked, and yet they are very good. There is nothing
disturbing about them; *ils peuvent être mis dans
toutes les mains;* they are kind, generous, even noble.
They sympathise with animate and inanimate nature.
They have shining foreheads with big bumps of
benevolence, like Flora Casby's father, and one
inclines to believe that their eyes must be frequently
filmed with an honest tear, if only because their vision
is blurred. They are fond of lists of names which
never suggest things; they are sparing of similes.
If they use them they are careful to see they are not
too definite, for a definite simile makes havoc of their
constructions, by applying to them a certain test of
reality.

But it is impossible to be serious about them.
The more stupid of them supply the matter for a good
laugh; the more clever the stuff of a more recondite
amazement. What *is* one to do when Mr Monro
apostrophises the force of Gravity in such words as
these ?—

' By leave of you man places stone on stone;
He scatters seed: you are at once the prop

Among the long roots of his fragile crop
You manufacture for him, and insure
House, harvest, implement, and furniture,
And hold them all secure.'

We are not surprised to learn further that

' I rest my body on your grass,
And let my brain repose in you.'

All that remains to be said is that Mr Monro is fond
of dogs (' Can you smell the rose ? ' he says to
Dog: ' ah, no! ') and inclined to fish—both of which
are Georgian inclinations.

Then there is Mr Drinkwater with the enthusiasm
of the just man for moonlit apples—' moon-washed
apples of wonder '—and the righteous man's sense
of robust rhythm in this chorus from ' Lincoln ':—

' You who know the tenderness
Of old men at eve-tide,
  Coming from the hedgerows,
Coming from the plough,
  And the wandering caress
Of winds upon the woodside,
  When the crying yaffle goes
Underneath the bough.'

Mr Drinkwater, though he cannot write good doggerel,
is a very good man. In this poem he refers to the
Sermon on the Mount as ' the words of light From
the mountain-way.'

Mr Squire, who is an infinitely more able writer,

would make an excellent subject for a critical investigation into false simplicity. He would repay a very
close analysis, for he may deceive the elect in the same
way as, we suppose, he deceives himself. His poem
' Rivers ' seems to us a very curious example of the
faux bon. Not only is the idea derivative, but the
rhythmical treatment also. Here is Mr de la Mare:—

> ' Sweet is the music of Arabia
> In my heart, when out of dreams
> I still in the thin clear murk of dawn
> Descry her gliding streams;
> Hear her strange lutes on the green banks
> Ring loud with the grief and delight
> Of the dim-silked, dark-haired musicians
> In the brooding silence of night.
> They haunt me—her lutes and her forests;
> No beauty on earth I see
> But shadowed with that dream recalls
> Her loveliness to me:
> Still eyes look coldly upon me,
> Cold voices whisper and say—
> " He is crazed with the spell of far Arabia,
> They have stolen his wits away." '

And here is a verse from Mr Squire:—

> ' For whatever stream I stand by,
> And whatever river I dream of,
> There is something still in the back of my
> mind
> From very far away;

There is something I saw and see not,
A country full of rivers
That stirs in my heart and speaks to me
   More sure, more dear than they.

' And always I ask and wonder
(Though often I do not know it)
Why does this water not smell like water ? . . .'

To leave the question of reminiscence aside, how the
delicate vision of Mr de la Mare has been coarsened,
how commonplace his exquisite technique has
become in the hands of even a first-rate ability!
It remains to be added that Mr Squire is an amateur
of nature,—

' And skimming, fork-tailed in the evening air,
   When man first was were not the martens
      there ? '—

and a lover of dogs.

Mr Shanks, Mr W. J. Turner, and Mr Freeman
belong to the same order. They have considerable
technical accomplishment of the straightforward kind
—and no emotional content. One can find examples
of the disastrous simile in them all. They are all in
their degree pseudo-naïves. Mr Turner wonders in
this way:—

' It is strange that a little mud
   Should echo with sounds, syllables, and letters,
   Should rise up and call a mountain Popocatapetl,
   And a green-leafed wood Oleander.'

144

Of course Mr Turner does not really wonder; those four lines are proof positive of that. But what matters is not so much the intrinsic value of the gift as the kindly thought which prompted the giver. Mr Shanks's speciality is beauty. He also is an amateur of nature. He bids us: 'Hear the loud night-jar spin his pleasant note.' Of course, Mr Shanks cannot have heard a real night-jar. His description is proof of that. But again, it was a kindly thought. Mr Freeman is, like Mr Squire, a more interesting case, deserving detailed analysis. For the moment we can only recommend a comparison of his first and second poems in this book with 'Sabrina Fair' and 'Love in a Valley' respectively.

It is only when we are confronted with the strange blend of technical skill and an emotional void that we begin to hunt for reminiscences. Reminiscences are no danger to the real poet. He is the splendid borrower who lends a new significance to that which he takes. He incorporates his borrowing in the new thing which he creates; it has its being there and there alone. One can see the process in the one fine poem in *Wheels*, Mr Wilfred Owen's 'Strange Meeting':—

' It seemed that out of the battle I escaped
   Down some profound dull tunnel, long since
      scooped
   Through granites which Titanic wars had
      groined.
   Yet also there encumbered sleepers groaned,
   Too fast in thought or death to be be-
      stirred.

Then, as I probed them, one sprang up, and
    stared
With piteous recognition in fixed eyes,
Lifting distressful hands as if to bless.
And by his smile, I knew that sullen hall.
With a thousand fears that vision's face was
    grained;
Yet no blood reached there from the upper
    ground,
And no guns thumped, or down the flues made
    moan.
" Strange, friend," I said, " Here is no cause
    to mourn."
" None," said the other, " save the undone
    years,
The hopelessness. Whatever hope is yours,
Was my life also . . ." '

The poem which begins with these lines is, we believe,
the finest in these two books, both in intention and
achievement. Yet no one can mistake its source. It
comes, almost bodily, from the revised Induction to
' Hyperion.' The sombre imagination, the sombre
rhythm is that of the dying Keats; the creative
impulse is that of Keats.

    ' None can usurp this height, return'd that
        shade,
    But those to whom the miseries of the world
    Are misery, and will not let them rest.'

That is true, word by word, and line by line, of
Wilfred Owen's ' Strange Meeting.' It touches

great poetry by more than the fringe; even in its technique there is the hand of the master to be. Those monosyllabic assonances are the discovery of genius. We are persuaded that this poem by a boy like his great forerunner, who had the certainty of death in his heart, is the most magnificent expression of the emotional significance of the war that has yet been achieved by English poetry. By including it in his book, the editor of *Wheels* has done a great service to English letters.

Extravagant words, it may be thought. We appeal to the documents. Read *Georgian Poetry* and read ' Strange Meeting.' Compare Wilfred Owen's poem with the very finest things in the Georgian book— Mr Davies's ' Lovely Dames,' or Mr de la Mare's ' The Tryst,' or ' Fare Well,' or the twenty opening lines of Mr Abercrombie's disappointing poem. You will not find those beautiful poems less beautiful than they are; but you will find in ' Strange Meeting ' an awe, an immensity, an adequacy to that which has been most profound in the experience of a generation. You will, finally, have the standard that has been lost, and the losing of which makes the confusion of a book like *Georgian Poetry* possible, restored to you. You will remember three forgotten things—that poetry is rooted in emotion, and that it grows by the mastery of emotion, and that its significance finally depends upon the quality and comprehensiveness of the emotion. You will recognise that the tricks of the trade have never been and never will be discovered by which ability can conjure emptiness into meaning.

It seems hardly worth while to return to *Wheels*. Once the argument has been pitched on the plane of

'Strange Meeting,' the rest of the contents of the book become irrelevant. But for the sake of symmetry we will characterise the corporate flavour of the opposition as false sophistication. There are the same contemporary reminiscences. Compare Mr Osbert Sitwell's *English Gothic* with Mr T. S. Eliot's *Sweeney*; and you will detect a simple mind persuading itself that it has to deal with the emotions of a complex one. The spectacle is almost as amusing as that of the similar process in the Georgian book. Nevertheless, in general, the affected sophistication here is, as we have said, merely irritating; while the affected simplicity of the coalition is positively noxious. Miss Edith Sitwell's deliberate painted toys are a great deal better than painted canvas trees and fields, masquerading as real ones. In the poems of Miss Iris Tree a perplexed emotion manages to make its way through a chaotic technique. She represents the solid impulse which lies behind the opposition in general. This impulse she describes, though she is very, very far from making poetry of it, in these not uninteresting verses:—

'But since we are mere children of this age,
 And must in curious ways discover salvation
 I will not quit my muddled generation,
 But ever plead for Beauty in this rage.

'Although I know that Nature's bounty yields
 Unto simplicity a beautiful content,
 Only when battle breaks me and my strength is
      spent
 Will I give back my body to the fields.'

148

Present Condition of English Poetry

There is the opposition. Against the righteous man, the *mauvais sujet*. We sympathise with the *mauvais sujet*. If he is persistent and laborious enough, he may achieve poetry. But he must travel alone. In order to be loyal to your age you must make up your mind what your age is. To be muddled yourself is not loyalty, but treachery, even to a muddled generation. [DECEMBER, 1919.

The Nostalgia of Mr Masefield

MR MASEFIELD is gradually finding his way to his self-appointed end, which is the glorification of England in narrative verse. *Reynard the Fox* marks, we believe, the end of a stage in his progress to this goal. He has reached a point at which his mannerisms have been so subdued that they no longer sensibly impede the movement of his verse, a point at which we may begin to speak (though not too loud) of mastery. We feel that he now approaches what he desires to do with some certainty of doing it, so that we in our turn can approach some other questions with some hope of answering them.

The questions are various; but they radiate from and enter again into the old question whether what he is doing, and beginning to do well, is worth while doing, or rather whether it will have been worth while doing fifty years hence. For we have no doubt at all in our mind that, in comparison with the bulk of contemporary poetry, such work as *Reynard the Fox* is valuable. We may use the old rough distinction and ask first whether *Reynard the Fox* is durable in virtue of its substance, and second, whether it is durable in virtue of its form.

The glorification of England! There are some who would give their souls to be able to glorify her as she has been glorified, by Shakespeare, by Milton, by Wordsworth, and by Hardy. For an Englishman there is no richer inspiration, no finer theme; to have one's speech and thought saturated by the fragrance

150

of this lovely and pleasant land was once the birthright of English poets and novelists. But something has crept between us and it, dividing. Instead of an instinctive love, there is a conscious desire of England; instead of slow saturation, a desperate plunge into its mystery. The fragrance does not come at its own sweet will; we clutch at it. It does not enfold and pervade our most arduous speculations; no involuntary sweetness comes flooding in upon our confrontation of human destinies. Hardy is the last of that great line. If we long for sweetness—as we do long for it, and with how poignant a pain!—we must seek it out, like men who rush dusty and irritable from the babble and fever of the town. The rhythm of the earth never enters into their gait; they are like spies among the birds and flowers, like collectors of antique furniture in the haunts of peace. The Georgians snatch at nature; they are never part of it. And there is some element of this desperation in Mr Masefield. We feel in him an anxiety to load every rift with ore of this particular kind, a deliberate intention to emphasise that which is most English in the English country-side.

How shall we say it? It is not that he makes a parade of arcane knowledge. The word ' parade ' does injustice to his indubitable integrity. But we seem to detect behind his superfluity of technical, and at times archaic phrase, an unconscious desire to convince himself that he is saturated in essential Englishness, and we incline to think that even his choice of an actual subject was less inevitable than self-imposed. He would isolate the quality he would capture, have it more wholly within his grasp; yet, in some subtle way, it finally eludes him. The intention is in excess, and in the manner of its execution everything is (though often very subtly) in excess also. The music of English place-names, for instance, is too insistent; no one into whom they had entered with the English air itself would use them with so manifest an admiration.

Perhaps a comparison may bring definition nearer. The first part of Mr Masefield's poem, which describes the meet and the assembled persons one by one, recalls, not merely by the general cast of the subject, but by many actual turns of phrase, Chaucer's *Prologue*. Mr Masefield's parson has more than one point of resemblance to Chaucer's Monk:—

> ' An out-ryder, that loved venerye;
>   A manly man to ben an abbot able. . . .'

But it would take too long to quote both pictures. We may choose for our juxtaposition the Prioress and one of Mr Masefield's young ladies:—

> ' Behind them rode her daughter Belle,
>   A strange, shy, lovely girl, whose face
>   Was sweet with thought and proud with race,
>   And bright with joy at riding there.
>   She was as good as blowing air,
>   But shy and difficult to know.
>   The kittens in the barley-mow,
>   The setter's toothless puppies sprawling,
>   The blackbird in the apple calling,
>   All knew her spirit more than we.
>   So delicate these maidens be
>   In loving lovely helpless things.'

The Nostalgia of Mr Masefield

And here is the Prioress:—

> ' But for to speken of hir conscience,
> She was so charitable and so pitous,
> She wolde weepe if that she sawe a mous
> Caught in a trappe, if it were ded or bledde.
> Of smalle houndes had she, that she fed
> With rosted flesh, or milk, or wastel bread,
> But sore wepte she if oon of hem were ded
> Or if men smote it with a yerde smerte:
> And all was conscience and tendere herte. '
> Ful semely hir wympel pynched was;
> His nose tretys; hir eyen greye as glas;
> Hir mouth full small, and thereto soft and red,
> But sikerly she hadde a fair forhed.'

There is in the Chaucer a naturalness, a lack of emphasis, a confidence that the object will not fail to make its own impression, beside which Mr Masefield's demonstration and underlining seem almost *malsain*. How far outside the true picture now appears that ' blackbird in the apple calling,' and how tainted by the desperate *bergerie* of the Georgian era!

It is, we admit, a portentous experiment to make, to set Mr Masefield's prologue beside Chaucer's. But not only is it a tribute to Mr Masefield that he brought us to reading Chaucer over again, but the comparison is at bottom just. Chaucer is not what we understand by a great poet; he has none of the imaginative comprehension and little of the music that belong to one: but he has perdurable qualities. He is at home with his speech and at home with his world; by his side Mr Masefield seems nervous and uncertain about both. He belongs, in fact, to a race

153

(or a generation) of poets who have come to feel a necessity of overloading every rift with ore. The question is whether such a man can hope to express the glory and the fragrance of the English country-side.

Can there be an element of permanence in a poem of which the ultimate impulse is a *nostalgie de la boue* that betrays itself in line after line, a nostalgia so conscious of separation that it cannot trust that any associations will be evoked by an unemphasised appeal ? Mr Masefield, in his fervour to grasp at that which for all his love is still alien to him, seems almost to shovel English mud into his pages; he cannot (and rightly cannot) persuade himself that the scent of the mud will be there otherwise. For the same reason he must make his heroes like himself. Here, for example, is the first whip, Tom Dansey:—

> ' His pleasure lay in hounds and horses;
> He loved the Seven Springs water-courses,
> Those flashing brooks (in good sound grass,
> Where scent would hang like breath on glass).
> He loved the English country-side;
> The wine-leaved bramble in the ride,
> The lichen on the apple-trees,
> The poultry ranging on the lees,
> The farms, the moist earth-smelling cover,
> His wife's green grave at Mitcheldover,
> Where snowdrops pushed at the first thaw.
> Under his hide his heart was raw
> With joy and pity of these things. . . .'

That ' raw heart ' marks the outsider, the victim of nostalgia. Apart from the fact that it is a manifest artistic blemish to impute it to the first whip of a pack

154

of foxhounds, the language is such that it would be a mistake to impute it to anybody; and with that we come to the question of Mr Masefield's style in general.

As if to prove how rough indeed was the provisionally accepted distinction between substance and form, we have for a long while already been discussing Mr Masefield's style under a specific aspect. But the particular overstrain we have been examining is part of Mr Masefield's general condition. Overstrain is permanent with him. If we do not find it in his actual language (and, as we have said, he is ridding himself of the worst of his exaggerations) we are sure to find it in the very vitals of his artistic effort. He is seeking always to be that which he is not, to lash himself into the illusion of a certainty which he knows he can never wholly possess.

> ' From the Gallows Hill to the Kineton Copse
> There were ten ploughed fields, like ten full-
>   stops,
> All wet red clay, where a horse's foot
> Would be swathed, feet thick, like an ash-tree
>   root.
> The fox raced on, on the headlands firm,
> Where his swift feet scared the coupling worm;
> The rooks rose raving to curse him raw,
> He snarled a sneer at their swoop and caw.
> Then on, then on, down a half-ploughed field
> Where a ship-like plough drove glitter-keeled,
> With a bay horse near and a white horse
>   leading,
> And a man saying " Zook," and the red earth
>   bleeding.'

The rasp of exacerbation is not to be mistaken. It comes, we believe, from a consciousness of anæmia, a frenetic reaction towards what used, some years ago, to be called ' blood and guts.'

And here, perhaps, we have the secret of Mr Masefield and of our sympathy with him. His work, for all its surface robustness and right-thinking (which has at least the advantage that it will secure for this ' epic of fox-hunting ' a place in the library of every country house), is as deeply debilitated by reaction as any of our time. Its colour is hectic; its tempo feverish. He has sought the healing virtue where he believed it undefiled, in that miraculous English country whose magic (as Mr Masefield so well knows) is in Shakespeare, and whose strong rhythm is in Hardy. But the virtue eludes all conscious inquisition. The man who seeks it feverishly sees riot where there is peace. And may it not be, in the long run, that Mr Masefield would have done better not to delude himself into an identification he cannot feel, but rather to face his own disquiet where alone the artist can master it, in his consciousness ? We will not presume to answer, mindful that Mr Masefield may not recognise himself in our mirror, but we will content ourselves with recording our conviction that in spite of the almost heroic effort that has gone to its composition *Reynard the Fox* lacks all the qualities essential to durability. [JANUARY, 1920.

The Lost Legions

ONE day, we believe, a great book will be written, informed by the breath which moves the Spirits of Pity in Mr Hardy's *Dynasts*. It will be a delicate, yet undeviating record of the spiritual awareness of the generation that perished in the war. It will be a work of genius, for the essence that must be captured within it is volatile beyond belief, almost beyond imagination. We know of its existence by signs hardly more material than a dream-memory of beating wings or an instinctive, yet all but inexplicable refusal of that which has been offered us in its stead. The autobiographer-novelists have been legion, yet we turn from them all with a slow shake of the head. ' No, it was not that. Had we lost only that we could have forgotten. It was not that.'

No, it was the spirit that troubled, as in dream, the waters of the pool, some influence which trembled between silence and a sound, a precarious confidence, an unavowed quest, a wisdom that came not of years or experience, a dissatisfaction, a doubt, a devotion, some strange presentiment, it may have been, of the bitter years in store, in memory an ineffable, irrevocable beauty, a visible seal on the forehead of a generation.

> ' When the lamp is shattered
> The light in the dust lies dead—
> When the cloud is scattered
> The rainbow's glory is shed.
> When the lute is broken,
> Sweet tones are remembered not . . .'

Yet out of a thousand fragments this memory must be created anew in a form that will outlast the years, for it was precious. It was something that would vindicate an epoch against the sickening adulation of the hero-makers and against the charge of spiritual sterility; a light in whose gleam the bewildering non-achievements of the present age, the art which seems not even to desire to be art, the faith which seems not to desire to be faith, have substance and meaning. It was shot through and through by an impulse of paradox, an unconscious straining after the impossible, gathered into two or three tremulous years which passed too swiftly to achieve their own expression. Now, what remains of youth is cynical, is successful, publicly exploits itself. It was not cynical then.

Elements of the influence that was are remembered only if they lasted long enough to receive a name. There was Unanimism. The name is remembered; perhaps the books are read. But it will not be found in the books. They are childish, just as the English novels which endeavoured to portray the soul of the generation were coarse and conceited. Behind all the conscious manifestations of cleverness and complexity lay a fundamental candour of which only a flickering gleam can now be recaptured. It glints on a page of M. Romains's *Europe*; the memory of it haunts Wilfred Owen's poems; it touches Keeling's letters; it hovers over these letters of Charles Sorley.[1] From a hundred strange lurking-places it must be gathered by pious and sensitive fingers and withdrawn from under the very edge of the scythe-blade

[1] *The Letters of Charles Sorley.* (Cambridge University Press.)

158

of time, for if it wander longer without a habitation it will be lost for ever.

Charles Sorley was the youngest fringe of the strange unity that included him and men by ten years his senior. He had not, as they had, plunged with fantastic hopes and unspoken fears into the world. He had not learned the slogans of the day. But, seeing that the slogans were only a disguise for the undefined desires which inspired them he lost little and gained much thereby. The years at Oxford in which he would have taken a temporary sameness, a sameness in the long run protective and strengthening, were spared him. In his letters we have him unspoiled, as the sentimentalists would say—not yet with the distraction of protective colouring.

One who knew him better than the mere reader of his letters can pretend to know him declares that, in spite of his poems, which are among the most remarkable of those of the boy-poets killed in the war, Sorley would not have been a man of letters. The evidence of the letters themselves is heavy against the view; they insist upon being regarded as the letters of a potential writer. But a passionate interest in literature is not the inevitable prelude to a life as a writer, and although it is impossible to consider any thread in Sorley's letters as of importance comparable to that which joins the enthronement and dethronement of his literary idols, we shall regard it as the record of a movement of soul which might as easily find expression (as did Keeling's) in other than literary activities. It takes more than literary men to make a generation, after all.

And Sorley was typical above all in this, that,

passionate and penetrating as was his devotion to literature, he never looked upon it as a thing existing in and for itself. It was, to him and his kind, the satisfaction of an impulse other and more complex than the æsthetic. Art was a means and not an end to him, and it is perhaps the apprehension of this that has led one who endeavoured in vain to reconcile Sorley to Pater into rash prognostication. Sorley would never have been an artist in Pater's way; he belonged to his own generation, to which *l'art pour l'art* had ceased to have meaning. There had come a pause, a throbbing silence, from which art might have emerged, may even now after the appointed time arise, with strange validities undreamed of or forgotten. Let us not prophesy; let us be content with the recognition that Sorley's generation was too keenly, perhaps too disastrously aware of destinies, of

> ' the beating of the wings of Love
> Shut out from his creation,'

to seek the comfort of the ivory tower.

Sorley first appears before us radiant with the white-heat of a schoolboy enthusiasm for Masefield. Masefield is—how we remember the feeling!—the poet who has lived; his naked reality tears through ' the lace of putrid sentimentalism (educing the effeminate in man) which rotters like Tennyson and Swinburne have taught his (the superficial man's) soul to love.' It tears through more than Tennyson and Swinburne. The greatest go down before him.

' So you see what I think of John Masefield.

When I say that he has the rapidity, simplicity, nobility of Homer, with the power of drawing character, the dramatic truth to life of Shakespeare, along with a moral and emotional strength and elevation which is all his own, and therefore I am prepared to put him above the level of these two great men—I do not expect you to agree with me.'—(From a paper read at Marlborough, November, 1912.)

That was Sorley at seventeen, and that, it seems to us, is the quality of enthusiasm which should be felt by a boy of seventeen if he is to make his mark. It is infinitely more important to have felt that flaming enthusiasm for an idol who will be cast down than to have felt what we ought to feel for Shakespeare and Homer. The gates of heaven are opened by strange keys, but they must be our own.

Within six months Masefield had gone the way of all flesh. In a paper on *The Shropshire Lad* (May, 1913), curious both for critical subtlety and the faint taste of disillusion, Sorley was saying: ' His (Masefield's) return (to the earth) was purely emotional, and probably less interesting than the purely intellectual return of Meredith.' At the beginning of 1914, having gained a Scholarship at University College, Oxford, he went to Germany. Just before going he wrote:—

' I am just discovering Thomas Hardy. There are two methods of discovery. One is when Columbus discovers America. The other is when some one begins to read a famous author who has already run into seventy editions, and refuses to speak about anything else, and considers every one else who reads

the author's works his own special converts. Mine
is the second method. I am more or less Hardy-
drunk.'

The humorous exactness and detachment of the
description are remarkable, and we feel that there was
more than the supersession of a small by a great idol
in this second phase. By April he is at Jena, 'only
15 miles from Goethe's grave, whose inhabitant has
taken the place of Thomas Hardy (successor to
Masefield) as my favourite prophet.'

'I hope (if nothing else) before I leave Germany
to get a thorough hang of *Faust*. . . . The worst of
a piece like *Faust* is that it completely dries up any
creative instincts or attempts in oneself. There is
nothing that I have ever thought or ever read that
is not somewhere contained in it, and (what is worse)
explained in it.'

He had a sublime contempt for any one with whom he
was not drunk. He lumped together 'nasty old
Lyttons, Carlyles, and Dickenses.' And the intoxica-
tion itself was swift and fleeting. There was something
wrong with Goethe by July; it is his 'entirely
intellectual' life.

'If Goethe really died saying "more light," it
was very silly of him: what *he* wanted was more
warmth.'

And he writes home for Richard Jefferies, the man of
his own county—for through Marlborough he had
made himself the adopted son of the Wiltshire Downs.
162

'In the midst of my setting up and smashing of deities—Masefield, Hardy, Goethe—I always fall back on Richard Jefferies wandering about in the background. I have at least the tie of locality with him.'

A day or two after we incidentally discover that Meredith is up (though not on Olympus) from a denunciation of Browning on the queer non- (or super-) æsthetic grounds of which we have spoken:—

'There is much in B. I like. But my feeling towards him has (ever since I read his life) been that of his to the "Lost Leader." I cannot understand him consenting to live a purely literary life in Italy, or (worse still) consenting to be lionised by fashionable London society. And then I always feel that if less people read Browning, more would read Meredith (his poetry, I mean.)'

Then, while he was walking in the Moselle Valley, came the war. He had loved Germany, and the force of his love kept him strangely free from illusions; he was not the stuff that "our modern Elizabethans" are made of. The keen candour of spiritual innocence is in what he wrote while training at Shorncliffe:—

'For the joke of seeing an obviously just cause defeated, I hope Germany will win. It would do the world good, and show that real faith is not that which says "we *must* win for our cause is just," but that which says "our cause is just: therefore we can disregard defeat."' . . .

' England—I am sick of the sound of the word. In training to fight for England, I am training to fight for that deliberate hypocrisy, that terrible middle-class sloth of outlook and appalling " imaginative indolence " that has marked us out from generation to generation. . . . And yet we have the impudence to write down Germany (who with all their bigotry are at least seekers) as " Huns," because they are doing what every brave man ought to do and making experiments in morality. Not that I approve of the experiment in this particular case. Indeed I think that after the war all brave men will renounce their country and confess that they are strangers and pilgrims on the earth. " For they that say such things declare plainly that they seek a country." But all these convictions are useless for me to state since I have not had the courage of them. What a worm one is under the cart-wheels—big, clumsy, careless, lumbering cart-wheels—of public opinion. I might have been giving my mind to fight against Sloth and Stupidity: instead, I am giving my body (by a refinement of cowardice) to fight against the most enterprising nation in the world.'

The wise arm-chair patriots will shake their heads; but there is more wisdom of spirit in these words than in all the newspaper leaders written throughout the war. Sorley was fighting for more than he said; he was fighting for his Wiltshire Downs as well. But he fought in complete and utter detachment. He died too soon (in October, 1915), to suffer the cumulative torment of those who lasted into the long agony of 1917. There is little bitterness in his

164

letters; they have to the last always the crystal clarity
of the vision of the unbroken.

His intellectual evolution went on to the end. No
wonder that he found Rupert Brooke's sonnets
overpraised:—

' He is far too obsessed with his own sacrifice.
. . . It was not that " they " gave up anything of
that list he gives in one sonnet: but that the essence
of these things had been endangered by circumstances
over which he had no control, and he must fight to
recapture them. He has clothed his attitude in fine
words: but he has taken the sentimental attitude.'

Remember that a boy of nineteen is writing, and think
how keen is this criticism of Brooke's war sonnets; the
seeker condemns without pity one who has given
up the search. ' There is no such thing as a just war,'
writes this boy. ' What we are doing is casting out
Satan by Satan.' From this position Sorley never
flinched. Never for a moment was he renegade to
his generation by taking ' the sentimental attitude.'
Neither had he in him an atom of the narrowness
of the straiter sect.

Though space forbids, we will follow out his
progress to the last. We do not receive many such
gifts as this book; the authentic voice of those lost
legions is seldom heard. We can afford, surely, to
listen to it to the end. In November, 1914, Sorley
turns back to the Hardy of the poems. After rejecting
' the actual " Satires of Circumstance " ' as bad
poetry, and passing an incisive criticism on ' Men
who March away,' he continues:—

' I cannot help thinking that Hardy is the greatest artist of the English character since Shakespeare: and much of *The Dynasts* (except its historical fidelity) might be Shakespeare. But I value his lyrics as presenting himself (the self he does not obtrude into the comprehensiveness of his novels and *The Dynasts*) as truly, and with faults as well as strength visible in it, as any character in his novels. His lyrics have not the spontaneity of Shakespeare's or Shelley's: they are rough-hewn and jagged: but I like them, and they stick.'

A little later, having finished *The Egoist*,—

' I see now that Meredith belongs to that class of novelists with whom I do not usually get on so well (*e.g.* Dickens), who create and people worlds of their own so that one approaches the characters with amusement, admiration, or contempt, not with liking or pity, as with Hardy's people, into whom the author does not inject his own exaggerated characteristics.'

The great Russians were unknown to Sorley when he died. What would he not have found in those mighty seekers, with whom Hardy alone stands equal ? But whatever might have been his vicissitudes in that strange company, we feel that Hardy could never have been dethroned in his heart, for other reasons than that the love of the Wessex hills had crept into his blood. He was killed on October 13, 1915, shot in the head by a sniper as he led his company at the ' hair-pin ' trench near Hulluch.

[JANUARY, 1920.

The Cry in the Wilderness

WE have in Mr Irving Babbitt's *Rousseau and Romanticism* to deal with a closely argued and copiously documented indictment of the modern mind. We gather that this book is but the latest of several books in which the author has gradually developed his theme, and we regret exceedingly that the preceding volumes have not fallen into our hands, because whatever may be our final attitude towards the author's conclusions, we cannot but regard *Rousseau and Romanticism* as masterly. Its style is, we admit, at times rather harsh and crabbed, but the critical thought which animates it is of a kind so rare that we are almost impelled to declare that it is the only book of modern criticism which can be compared for clarity and depth of thought with Mr Santayana's *Three Philosophical Poets*.

By endeavouring to explain the justice of that verdict we shall more easily give an indication of the nature and scope of Professor Babbitt's achievement. We think that it would be easy to show that in the last generation—we will go no further back for the moment, though our author's arraignment reaches at least a century earlier—criticism has imperceptibly given way to a different activity which we may call appreciation. The emphasis has been laid upon the uniqueness of the individual, and the unconscious or avowed aim of the modern ' critic ' has been to persuade us to understand, to sympathise with and in the last resort to enter into the whole psychological process which culminated in the artistic creation of the author examined. And there modern criticism has stopped. There has been no indication that it was aware of the necessity of going further. Many influences went to shape the general conviction that mere presentation was the final function of criticism, but perhaps the chief of these was the curious contagion of a scientific terminology. The word ' objectivity ' had a great vogue; it was felt that the spiritual world was analogous to the physical; the critic was faced, like the man of science, with a mass of hard, irreducible facts, and his function was, like the scientist's, that of recording them as compendiously as possible and without prejudice. The unconscious programme was, indeed, impossible of fulfilment. All facts may be of equal interest to the scientist, but they are not to the literary critic. He chose those which interested him most for the exercise of his talent for demonstration. But that choice was, as a general rule, the only specifically critical act which he performed, and, since it was usually unmotived, it was difficult to attach even to that more than a ' scientific ' importance. Reasoned judgments of value were rigorously eschewed, and even though we may presume that the modern critic is at times vexed by the problem why (or whether) one work of art is better than another, when each seems perfectly expressive of the artist's intention, the preoccupation is seldom betrayed in the language of his appreciation. Tacitly and insensibly we have reached a point at which all works of art are equally good if they are equally expressive. What every artist seeks to express is his own unique consciousness. As between things

168

unique there is no possibility of subordination or comparison.

That does not seem to us an unduly severe diagnosis of modern criticism, although it needs perhaps to be balanced by an acknowledgment that the impulse towards the penetration of an artist's consciousness is in itself salutary, as a valuable adjunct to the methods of criticism, provided that it is definitely subordinated to the final critical judgment, before which uniqueness is an impossible plea. Such a diagnosis will no doubt be welcomed by those who belong to an older generation than that to which it is applied. But they should not rejoice prematurely. We require of them an answer to the question whether they were really in better case—whether they were not the fathers whose sins are visited upon the children. Professor Babbitt, at least, has no doubt of their responsibility. From his angle of approach we might rake their ranks with a cross-fire of questions such as these: When you invoked the sanction of criticism were you more than merely destructive? When you riddled religion with your scientific objections, did you not forget that religion is something more, far more than a nexus of historical facts or a cosmogony? When you questioned everything in the name of truth and science, why did you not dream of asking whether those creations of men's minds were *capax imperii* in man's universe? What right had you to suppose that a man disarmed of tradition is stronger for his nakedness? Why did you not examine in the name of that same truth and science the moral nature of man, and see whether it was fit to bear the burden of intolerable knowledge which you put upon it?

169

Why did you, the truth-seekers and the scientists, indulge yourselves in the most romantic dream of a natural man who followed instinctively the greatest good of the greatest number, which you yourselves never for one moment pursued ? What hypocrisy or self-deception enabled you to clothe your statements of fact in a moral aura, and to blind yourselves and the world to the truth that you were killing a domesticated dragon who guarded the cave of a devouring hydra, whom you benevolently loosed ? Why did you not see that the end of all your devotion was to shift man's responsibility for himself from his shoulders ? Do you, because you clothed yourselves in the shreds of a moral respectability which you had not the time (or was it the courage ?) to analyse, dare to denounce us because our teeth are set on edge by the sour grapes which you enjoyed ?

But this indictment, it may be said by a modern critic, deals with morals, and we are discussing art and criticism. That the objection is conceivable is precisely the measure of our decadence. For the vital centre of our ethics is also the vital centre of our art. Moral nihilism inevitably involves an æsthetic nihilism, which can be obscured only temporarily by an insistence upon technical perfection as in itself a supreme good. Neither the art of religion nor the religion of art is an adequate statement of the possibilities and purpose of art, but there is no doubt that the religion of art is by far the more vacuous of the two. The values of literature, the standards by which it must be criticised, and the scheme according to which it must be arranged, are in the last resort moral. The sense that they should be more moral than morality

170

The Cry in the Wilderness

affords no excuse for accepting them when they are less so. Literature should be a kingdom where a sterner morality, a more strenuous liberty prevails —where the artist may dispense if he will with the ethics of the society in which he lives, but only on condition of revealing a deeper insight into the moral law to whose allegiance man, in so far as he is man and not a beast, inevitably tends. Never, we suppose, was an age in which art stood in greater need of the true law of decorum than this. Its philosophy has played it false. It has passed from the nebulous Hegelian adulation of the accomplished fact (though one would have thought that to a generation with even a vague memory of Aristotle's *Poetics*, the mere title, *The Philosophy of History* would have been an evident danger signal) to an adulation of science and of instinct. From one side comes the cry, ' Man *is* a beast '; from the other, ' Trust your instincts.' The sole manifest employment of reason is to overthrow itself. Yet it should be, in conjunction with the imagination, the vital principle of control.

Professor Babbitt would have us back to Aristotle, or back to our senses, which is roughly the same thing. At all events, it is certain that in Aristotle the present generation would find the beginnings of a remedy for that fatal confusion of categories which has overcome the world. It is the confusion between existence and value. That strange malady of the mind by which in the nineteenth century material progress was supposed to create, *ipso facto*, a concomitant moral progress, and which so plunged the world into catastrophe, has its counterpart in a literature of objective realism. One of the most

171

admired of contemporary works of fiction opens with
an infant's memory of a mackintosh sheet, pleasantly
warmed with its own water; another, of almost equal
popularity among the cultivated, abounds with such
reminiscences of the heroine as the paste of bread
with which she filled her decaying teeth while she
ate her breakfast. Yet the young writers who abuse
their talents so unspeakably have right on their side
when they refuse to listen to the condemnation pro-
nounced by an older generation. What right, indeed,
have these to condemn the logical outcome of an
anarchic individualism which they themselves so
jealously cherished ? They may not like the bastard
progeny of the various mistresses they adored—of a
Science which they enthroned above instead of
subordinating to humanistic values, of a brutal
Imperialism which the so-called Conservatives among
them set up in place of the truly humane devotion of
which man is capable, of the sickening humanitarianism
which appears in retrospect to have been merely an
excuse for absolute indolence—but they certainly have
forfeited the right to censure it. Let those who are
so eager to cast the first stone at the æsthetic and
moral anarchy of the present day consider Professor
Babbitt's indictment of themselves and decide whether
they have no sin :—

' " If I am to judge by myself," said an eighteenth-
century Frenchman, "man is a stupid animal."
Man is not only a stupid animal, in spite of his conceit
of his own cleverness, but we are here at the source
of his stupidity. The source is the moral indolence
that Buddha, with his almost infallible sagacity,

172

defined long ago. In spite of the fact that his spiritual and, in the long run, his material success, hinge on his ethical effort, man persists in dodging this effort, in seeking to follow the line of least or lesser resistance. An energetic material working does not mend, but aggravate the failure to work ethically, and is therefore especially stupid. Just this combination has in fact led to the crowning stupidity of the ages—the Great War. No more delirious spectacle has ever been witnessed than that of hundreds of millions of human beings using a vast machinery of scientific efficiency to turn life into a hell for one another. It is hard to avoid concluding that we are living in a world which has gone wrong on first principles, a world that, in spite of all the warnings of the past, has allowed itself to be caught once more in the terrible naturalistic trap. The dissolution of civilisation with which we are threatened is likely to be worse in some respects than that of Greece or Rome, in view of the success that has been obtained in 'perfecting the mystery of murder.' Various traditional agencies are indeed still doing much to chain up the beast in man. Of these the chief is no doubt the Church. But the leadership of the Occident is no longer here. The leaders have succumbed in greater or less degree to naturalism, and so have been tampering with the moral law. That the brutal imperialist who brooks no obstacle to his lust for domination has been tampering with this law goes without saying, but the humanitarian, all adrip with brotherhood and profoundly convinced of the loveliness of his own soul, has been tampering with it also, and in a more dangerous way, for the very reason that it is less obvious. This tampering with the moral law, or, what amounts to the same thing, this overriding of the veto power in man, has been largely a result, though not a necessary result, of the rupture with the traditional forms of wisdom. The Baconian naturalist repudiated the past because he wished to be more positive and critical, to plant himself on the facts. But the veto power is itself a fact—the weightiest with which man has to reckon. The Rousseauistic naturalist threw off traditional control because he wished to be more imaginative. Yet without the veto power imagination falls into sheer anarchy. Both Baconian and Rousseauist were very impatient of any outer authority that seemed to stand between them and their own perceptions. Yet the veto power is nothing abstract, nothing that one needs to take on hearsay, but is very immediate. The naturalistic leaders may be proved wrong without going beyond their own principles, and their wrongness is of a kind to wreck civilisation.'

We find it impossible to refuse our assent to the main counts of this indictment. The deanthropocentrised universe of science is not the universe in which man has to live. That universe is at once smaller and larger than the universe of science: smaller in material extent, larger in spiritual possibility. Therefore to allow the perspective of science seriously to influence, much less control, our human values, is an invitation to disaster. Humanism must reassert itself, for even we can see that Shakespeares are better than Hamlets. The reassertion of humanism involves the re-creation of a practical ideal of human life and

174

conduct, and a strict subordination of the impulses of the individual to this ideal. There must now be a period of critical and humanistic positivism in regard to ethics and to art. We may say frankly that it is not to our elders that we think of applying for its rudiments. We regard them as no less misguided and a good deal less honest than ourselves. It is among our anarchists that we shall look most hopefully for our new traditionalists, if only because, in literature at least, they are more keenly aware of the nature of the abyss on the brink of which they are trembling. [FEBRUARY, 1920.

Poetry and Criticism

NOWADAYS we are all vexed by this question of poetry, and in ways peculiar to ourselves. Fifty years ago the dispute was whether Browning was a greater poet than Tennyson or Swinburne; to-day it is apparently more fundamental, and perhaps substantially more threadbare. We are in a curious, half-conscious way incessantly debating what poetry is, impelled by a sense that, although we have been living at a time of extraordinarily prolific poetic production, not very much good has come out of it. Having thus passed the stage at which the theory that poetry is an end in itself will suffice us, we vaguely cast about in our minds for some fuller justification of the poetic activity. A presentiment that our poetic values are chaotic is widespread; we are uncomfortable with it, and there is, we believe, a genuine desire that a standard should be once more created and applied.

What shall we require of poetry? Delight, music, subtlety of thought, a world of the heart's desire, fidelity to comprehensible experience, a glimpse through magic casements, profound wisdom? All these things—all different, yet not all contradictory —have been required of poetry. What shall we require of her? The answer comes, it seems, as quick and as vague as the question. We require the highest. All that can be demanded of any spiritual activity of man we must demand of poetry. It must be adequate to all our experience; it must be

176

not a diversion from, but a culmination of life; it must be working steadily towards a more complete universality.

Suddenly we may turn upon ourselves and ask what right we have to demand these things of poetry; or others will turn upon us and say: ' This is a lyrical age.' To ourselves and to the others we are bound to reply that poetry must be maintained in the proud position where it has always been, the sovereign language of the human spirit, the sublimation of all experience. In the past there has never been a lyrical age, though there have been ages of minor poetry, when poetry was no longer deliberately made the vehicle of man's profoundest thought and most searching experience. Nor was it the ages of minor poetry which produced great lyrical poetry. Great lyrical poetry has always been an incidental achievement, a parergon, of great poets, and great poets have always been those who believed that poetry was by nature the worthiest vessel of the highest argument of which the soul of man is capable.

Yet a poetic theory such as this seems bound to include great prose, and not merely the prose which can most easily be assimilated to the condition of poetry, such as Plato's *Republic* or Milton's *Areopagitica*, but the prose of the great novelists. Surely the colloquial prose of Tchehov's *Cherry Orchard* has as good a claim to be called poetry as *The Essay on Man*, *Tess of the D'Urbervilles* as *The Ring and the Book*, *The Possessed* as *Phèdre*? Where are we to call a halt in the inevitable process by which the kinds of literary art merge into one?

If we insist that rhythm is essential to poetry, we are in danger of confusing the accident with the essence, and of fastening upon what will prove to be in the last analysis a merely formal difference. The difference we seek must be substantial and essential.

The very striking merit of Sir Henry Newbolt's *New Study of English Poetry* is that he faces the ultimate problem of poetry with courage, sincerity, and an obvious and passionate devotion to the highest spiritual activity of man. It has seldom been our good fortune to read a book of criticism in which we were so impressed by what we can only call a purity of intention; we feel throughout that the author's aim is single, to set before us the results of his own sincere thinking on a matter of infinite moment. Perhaps better, because subtler, books of literary criticism have appeared in England during the last ten years—if so, we have not read them; but there has been none more truly tolerant, more evidently free from malice, more certainly the product of a soul in which no lie remains. Whether it is that Sir Henry has like Plato's Cephalus lived his literary life blamelessly, we do not know, but certainly he produces upon us an effect akin to that of Cephalus's peaceful smile when he went on his way to sacrifice duly to the gods and left the younger men to the intricacies of their infinite debate.

Now it seems to us of importance that a writer like Sir Henry Newbolt should declare roundly that creative poetry and creative prose belong to the same kind. It is important not because there is anything

178

very novel in the contention, but because it is opportune; and it is opportune because at the present
moment we need to have emphasis laid on the vital
element that is common both to creative poetry and
creative prose. The general mind loves confusion,
blest mother of haze and happiness; it loves to be
able to conclude that this is an age of poetry from the
fact that the books of words cut up into lines or
sprinkled with rhymes are legion. An age of fiddle-
sticks! Whatever the present age is—and it is an
age of many interesting characteristics—it is not an
age of poetry. It would indeed have a better chance
of being one if fifty instead of five hundred books of
verse were produced every month; and if all the
impresarios were shouting that it was an age of prose.
The differentia of verse is a merely trivial accident;
what is essential in poetry, or literature if you will, is
an act of intuitive comprehension. Where you have
the evidence of that act, the sovereign æsthetic process,
there you have poetry. What remains for you, whether
you are a critic or a poet or both together, is to settle
for yourself a system of values by which those various
acts of intuitive comprehension may be judged. It
does not suffice at any time, much less does it suffice
at the present day, to be content with the uniqueness
of the pleasure which you derive from each single act
of comprehension made vocal. That contentment is
the comfortable privilege of the amateur and the
dilettante. It is not sufficient to get a unique pleasure
from Mr De la Mare's *Arabia* or Mr Davies's *Lovely
Dames* or Miss Katherine Mansfield's *Prelude* or Mr
Eliot's *Portrait of a Lady*, in each of which the vital
act of intuitive comprehension is made manifest.

One must establish a hierarchy, and decide which act of comprehension is the more truly comprehensive, which poem has the completer universality. One must be prepared not only to relate each poetic expression to the finest of its kind in the past, or to recognise a new kind if a new kind has been created, but to relate the kind to the finest kind.

That, as it seems to us, is the specifically critical activity, and one which is in peril of death from desuetude. The other important type of criticism, which is analysis of poetic method, an investigation and appreciation of the means by which the poet communicates his intuitive comprehension to an audience, is in a less perilous condition. Where there are real poets—and only a bigot will deny that there are real poets among us now: we have just named four—there will always be true criticism of poetic method, though it may seldom find utterance in the printed word. But criticism of poetic method has, by hypothesis, no perspective and no horizons; it is concerned with a unique thing under the aspect of its uniqueness. It may, and happily most often does, assume that poetry is the highest expression of the spiritual life of man; but it makes no endeavour to assess it according to the standards that are implicit in such an assumption. That is the function of philosophical criticism. If philosophical criticism can be combined with criticism of method—and there is no reason why they should not coexist in a single person; the only two English critics of the nineteenth century, Coleridge and Arnold, were of this kind —so much the better; but it is philosophical criticism of which we stand in desperate need at this moment.

A good friend of ours, who happens to be one of the few real poets we possess, once wittily summed up a general objection to criticism of the kind we advocate as 'always asking people to do what they can't.' But to point out, as the philosophical critic would, that poetry itself must inevitably languish if the more comprehensive kinds are neglected, or if a non-poetic age is allowed complacently to call itself lyrical, is not to urge the real masters in the less comprehensive kinds to desert their work. Who but a fool would ask Mr De la Mare to write an epic or Miss Mansfield to give us a novel ? But he might be a wise man who called upon Mr Eliot to set himself to the composition of a poetic drama; and without a doubt he would deserve well of the commonwealth who should summon the popular imitators of Mr De la Mare, Mr Davies, or Mr Eliot to begin by trying to express something that they did comprehend or desired to comprehend, even though it should take them into thousands of unprintable pages. It is infinitely preferable that those who have so far given evidence of nothing better than a fatal fluency in insipid imitation of true lyric poets should fall down a precipice in the attempt to scale the very pinnacles of Parnassus. There is something heroic about the most unmitigated disaster at such an altitude.

Moreover, the most marked characteristic of the present age is a continual disintegration of the consciousness; more or less deliberately in every province of man's spiritual life the reins are being thrown on to the horse's neck. The power which controls and

disciplines sensational experience is, in modern literature, daily denied; the counterpart of this power
which envisages the ideal in the conduct of one's
own or the nation's affairs and unfalteringly pursues
it is held up to ridicule. Opportunism in politics
has its complement in opportunism in poetry. Mr
Lloyd George's moods are reflected in Mr ———'s.
And, beneath these heights, we have the queer
spectacle of a whole race of very young poets who
somehow expect to attain poetic intensity by the
physical intensity with which they look at any disagreeable object that happens to come under their
eye. Perhaps they will find some satisfaction in being
reckoned among the curiosities of literature a hundred
years hence; it is certainly the only satisfaction they
will have. They, at any rate, have a great deal to
gain from the acid of philosophical criticism. If a
reaction to life has in itself the seeds of an intuitive
comprehension it will stand explication. If a young
poet's nausea at the sight of a toothbrush is significant
of anything at all except bad upbringing, then it is
capable of being refined into a vision of life and of
being expressed by means of the appropriate mechanism
or myth. But to register the mere facts of consciousness, undigested by the being, without assessment
or reinforcement by the mind is, for all the connection
it has with poetry, no better than to copy down the
numbers of one's bus-tickets.

We do not wish to suggest that Sir Henry Newbolt
would regard this lengthy gloss upon his book as
legitimate deduction. He, we think, is a good deal
more tolerant than we are; and he would probably
hesitate to work out the consequences of the principles

which he enunciates and apply them vigorously to the present time. But as a vindication of the supreme place of poetry as poetry in human life, as a stimulus to critical thought and a guide to exquisite appreciation—of which his essay on Chaucer is an honourable example—*A New Study of English Poetry* deserves all the praise that lies in our power to give.

[MARCH, 1920.

Coleridge's Criticism

IT is probably true that *Biographia Literaria* is the best book of criticism in the English language; nevertheless, it is rash to assume that it is a book of criticism of the highest excellence, even when it has passed through the salutary process of drastic editing, such as that to which, in the present case,[1] the competent hands of Mr George Sampson have submitted it. Its garrulity, its digressions, its verbiage, the marks which even the finest portions show of submersion in the tepid transcendentalism that wrought such havoc upon Coleridge's mind—these are its familiar disfigurements. They are not easily removed; for they enter fairly deeply even in the texture of those portions of the book in which Coleridge devotes himself, as severely as he can, to the proper business of literary criticism.

It may be that the prolixity with which he discusses and refutes the poetical principles expounded by Wordsworth in the preface of *Lyrical Ballads* was due to the tenderness of his consideration for Wordsworth's feelings, an influence to which Sir Arthur Quiller-Couch directs our attention in his introduction. That is honourable to Coleridge as a man; but it cannot exculpate him as a critic. For the points he had to make for and against Wordsworth were few and simple. First, he had to show that the theory

[1] *Coleridge* : *Biographia Literaria*, Chapters I.-IV., XIV.-XXII. —*Wordsworth* : *Prefaces and Essays on Poetry*, 1800-1815. Edited by George Sampson, with an Introductory Essay by Sir Arthur Quiller-Couch. (Cambridge University Press.)

of a poetic diction drawn exclusively from the language of ' real life ' was based upon an equivocation, and therefore was useless. This Coleridge had to show to clear himself of the common condemnation in which he had been involved, as one wrongly assumed to endorse Wordsworth's theory. He had an equally important point to make for Wordsworth. He wished to prove to him that the finest part of his poetic achievement was based upon a complete neglect of this theory, and that the weakest portions of his work were those in which he most closely followed it. In this demonstration he was moved by the desire to set his friend on the road that would lead to the most triumphant exercise of his own powers.

There is no doubt that Coleridge made both his points; but he made them, in particular the former, at exceeding length, and at the cost of a good deal of internal contradiction. He sets out, in the former case, to maintain that the language of poetry is essentially different from the language of prose. This he professes to deduce from a number of principles. His axiom—and it is possibly a sound one—is that metre originated in a spontaneous effort of the mind to hold in check the workings of emotion. From this, he argues, it follows that to justify the existence of metre, the language of a poem must show evidence of emotion, by being different from the language of prose. Further, he says, metre in itself stimulates the emotions, and for this condition of emotional excitement ' correspondent food ' must be provided. Thirdly, the emotion of poetical composition itself demands this same ' correspondent food.' The final argument, if we omit one drawn from an obscure theory of imitation very characteristic of Coleridge, is the incontrovertible appeal to the authority of the poets.

Unfortunately, the elaborate exposition of the first three arguments is not only unnecessary but confusing, for Coleridge goes on to distinguish, interestingly enough, between a language proper to poetry, a language proper to prose, and a neutral language which may be used indifferently in prose and poetry, and later still he quotes a beautiful passage from Chaucer's *Troilus and Cressida* as an example of this neutral language, forgetting that, if his principles are correct, Chaucer was guilty of a sin against art in writing *Troilus and Cressida* in metre. The truth, of course, is that the paraphernalia of principles goes by the board. In order to refute the Wordsworthian theory of a language of real life supremely fitted for poetry you have only to point to the great poets, and to judge the fitness of the language of poetry you can only examine the particular poem. Wordsworth was wrong and self-contradictory without doubt; but Coleridge was equally wrong and self-contradictory in arguing that metre *necessitated* a language essentially different from that of prose.

So it is that the philosophic part of the specifically literary criticism of the *Biographia* takes us nowhere in particular. The valuable part is contained in his critical appreciation of Wordsworth's poetry and that amazing chapter—a little forlorn, as most of Coleridge's fine chapters are—on ' the specific symptoms of poetic power elucidated in a critical analysis of Shakespeare's *Venus and Adonis*. In these few pages Coleridge is at the summit of his powers as a critic. So long as his

186

attention could be fixed on a particular object, so long as he was engaged in deducing his general principles immediately from particular instances of the highest kind of poetic excellence, he was a critic indeed. Every one of the four points characteristic of early poetic genius which he formulates deserves to be called back to the mind again and again:—

' The delight in richness and sweetness of sound, even to a faulty excess, if it be evidently original and not the result of an easily imitable mechanism, I regard as a highly favourable promise in the compositions of a young man. . . .

' A second promise of genius is the choice of subjects very remote from the private interests and circumstances of the writer himself. At least I have found, that where the subject is taken immediately from the author's personal sensations and experiences the excellence of a particular poem is but an equivocal mark, and often a fallacious pledge, of genuine poetical power. . . .

' Images, however beautiful, though faithfully copied from nature, and as accurately represented in words, do not of themselves characterise the poet. They become proofs of original genius only as far as they are modified by a predominant passion; or by associated thoughts or images awakened by that passion; or when they have the effect of reducing multitude to unity, or succession to an instant; or lastly, when a human and intellectual life is transferred to them from the poet's own spirit. . . .

' The last character . . . which would prove

indeed but little, except as taken conjointly with the former—yet without which the former could scarce exist in a high degree . . . is *depth*, and *energy* of *thought*. No man was ever yet a great poet without being at the same time a profound philosopher. For poetry is the blossom and the fragrancy of all human knowledge, human thoughts, human passions, emotions, language.'

In the context the most striking peculiarity of this enunciation of the distinguishing marks of poetic power, apart from the conviction which it brings, is that they are not in the least concerned with the actual language of poetry. The whole subject of poetic diction is dropped when Coleridge's critical, as opposed to his logical, faculty is at work; and, although this Chapter XV is followed by many pages devoted to the analysis and refutation of the Wordsworthian theory and to the establishment of those principles of poetic diction to which we have referred, when Coleridge comes once more to engage his pure critical faculty, in the appreciation of Wordsworth's actual poetry in Chapter XXII, we again find him ignoring his own principles precisely on those occasions when we might have thought them applicable.

Coleridge enumerates Wordsworth's defects one by one. The first, he says, is an inconstancy of style. For a moment he appears to invoke his principles : ' Wordsworth sinks too often and too abruptly to that style which I should place in the second division of language, dividing it into the three species; *first*, that which is peculiar to poetry; *second*, that which is proper only in prose; and *third*, the neutral or common

188

to both.' But in the very first instance which Coleridge gives we can see that the principles have been dragged in by the hair, and that they are really alien to the argument which he is pursuing. He gives this example of disharmony from the poem on ' The Blind Highland Boy ' (whose washing-tub in the 1807 edition, it is perhaps worth noting, had been changed at Coleridge's own suggestion, with a rash contempt of probabilities, into a turtle shell in the edition of 1815):—

   ' And one, the rarest, was a shell
     Which he, poor child, had studied well:
     The Shell of a green Turtle, thin
     And hollow;—you might sit therein,
       It was so wide, and deep.

   ' Our Highland Boy oft visited
     The house which held this prize; and led
     By choice or chance, did thither come
     One day, when no one was at home,
       And found the door unbarred.'

    The discord is, in any case, none too apparent; but if one exists, it does not in the least arise from the actual language which Wordsworth has used. If in anything, it consists in a slight shifting of the focus of apprehension, a sudden and scarcely perceptible emphasis on the detail of actual fact, which is a deviation from the emotional key of the poem as a whole. In the next instance the lapse is, however, indubitable:—

' Thou hast a nest, for thy love and thy rest,
And though little troubled with sloth,
Drunken Lark! thou would'st be loth
To be such a traveller as I.
Happy, happy liver!
With a soul as strong as a mountain River
Pouring out praise to th' Almighty Giver,
Joy and jollity be with us both,
Hearing thee or else some other
As merry as a Brother
I on the earth will go plodding on,
By myself, cheerfully, till the day is done.'

The two lines in italics are discordant. But again it is no question of language in itself; it is an internal discrepancy between the parts of a whole already debilitated by metrical insecurity.

Coleridge's second point against Wordsworth is ' a *matter-of-factness* in certain poems.' Once more there is no question of language. Coleridge takes the issue on to the highest and most secure ground. Wordsworth's obsession with realistic detail is a contravention of the essential catholicity of poetry; and this accidentality is manifested in laboriously exact description both of places and persons. The poet sterilises the creative activity of poetry, in the first case, for no reason at all, and in the second, because he proposes as his immediate object a moral end instead of the giving of æsthetic pleasure. His prophets and wise men are pedlars and tramps not because it is probable that they should be of this condition—it is on the contrary highly improbable —but because we are thus to be taught a salutary

moral lesson. The question of language in itself, if it
enters at all here, enters only as the indifferent means
by which a non-poetic end is sought. The accidentality
lies not in the words, but in the poet's intention.

Coleridge's third and fourth points, ' an undue
predilection for the dramatic form,' and ' an eddying
instead of a progression of thought,' may be passed
as quickly as he passes them himself, for in any case
they could only be the cause of a jejuneness of language. The fifth, more interesting, is the appearance
of ' thoughts and images too great for the subject
. . . an approximation to what might be called
mental bombast.' Coleridge brings forward as his
first instance of this four lines which have taken a
deep hold on the affections of later generations:—

> ' They flash upon the inward eye
> Which is the bliss of solitude!
> And then my heart with pleasure fills
> And dances with the daffodils.'

Coleridge found an almost burlesque bathos in the
second couplet after the first. It would be difficult
for a modern critic to accept that verdict altogether;
nevertheless his objection to the first couplet as a
description of physical vision is surely sound. And
it is interesting to note that the objection has been
evaded by posterity in a manner which confirms
Coleridge's criticism. The ' inward eye ' is almost
universally remembered apart from its context, and
interpreted as a description of the purely spiritual
process to which alone, in Coleridge's opinion, it was
truly apt.

The enumeration of Wordsworth's excellences which follows is masterly; and the exhilaration with which one rises through the crescendo to the famous: ' Last and pre-eminently, I challenge for this poet the gift of *Imagination* in the highest and strictest sense of the word . . .' is itself a pleasure to be derived only from the gift of criticism of the highest and strictest kind.

The object of this examination has been to show, not that the *Biographia Literaria* is undeserving of the high praise which has been bestowed upon it, but that the praise has been to some extent undiscriminating. It has now become almost a tradition to hold up to our admiration Coleridge's chapter on poetic diction, and Sir Arthur Quiller-Couch, in a preface that is as unconventional in manner as it is stimulating in most of its substance, maintains the tradition. As a matter of fact, what Coleridge has to say on poetic diction is prolix and perilously near commonplace. Instead of making to Wordsworth the wholly sufficient answer that much poetry of the highest kind employs a language that by no perversion can be called essentially the same as the language of prose, he allows himself to be led by his German metaphysic into considering poetry as a *Ding an sich* and deducing therefrom the proposition that poetry *must* employ a language different from that of prose. That proposition is false, as Coleridge himself quite adequately shows from his remarks upon what he called the ' neutral ' language of Chaucer and Herbert. But instead of following up the clue and beginning to inquire whether or not narrative poetry by nature demands a language approximating to that of prose, and whether Wordsworth, in so far as he aimed at being a narrative poet, was not working on a correct but exaggerated principle, he leaves the bald contradiction and swerves off to the analysis of the defects and excellences of Wordsworth's actual achievement. Precisely because we consider it of the greatest importance that the best of Coleridge's criticism should be studied and studied again, we think it unfortunate that Sir Arthur Quiller-Couch should recommend the apprentice to get the chapters on poetic diction by heart. He will be condemned to carry about with him a good deal of dubious logic and a false conclusion. What is worth while learning from Coleridge is something different; it is not his behaviour with ' a principle,' but his conduct when confronted with poetry in the concrete, his magisterial ordonnance (to use his own word) and explication of his own æsthetic intuitions, and his manner of employing in this, the essential task of poetic criticism, the results of his own deep study of all the great poetry that he knew. [APRIL, 1920.

Shakespeare Criticism

IT is an exciting, though exhausting, experience to read a volume of the great modern Variorum Shakespeare from cover to cover. One derives from the exercise a sense of the evolution of Shakespeare criticism which cannot be otherwise obtained; one begins to understand that Pope had his merits as an editor, as indeed a man of genius could hardly fail to have, to appreciate the prosy and pedestrian pains of Theobald, to admire the amazing erudition of Steevens. One sees the phases of the curious process by which Shakespeare was elevated at the beginning of the nineteenth century to a sphere wherein no mortal man of genius could breathe. For a dizzy moment every line that he wrote bore the authentic impress of the divine. *Efflavit deus.* In a century, from being largely beneath criticism Shakespeare had passed to a condition where he was almost completely beyond it.

King John affords an amusing instance of this reverential attitude. The play, as is generally known, was based upon a slightly earlier and utterly un-Shakespearean production entitled *The Troublesome Raigne of King John.* The only character Shakespeare added to those he found ready to his hand was that of James Gurney, who enters with Lady Falconbridge after the scene between the Bastard and his brother, says four words, and departs for ever.

194

' *Bast.*—James Gurney, wilt thou give us leave
awhile ?
Gur.—Good leave, good Philip.
Bast.—Philip ! Sparrow! James.'

It is obvious that Shakespeare's sole motive in
introducing Gurney is to provide an occasion for
the Bastard's characteristic, though not to a modern
mind quite obvious, jest, based on the fact that
Philip was at the time a common name for a sparrow.
The Bastard, just dubbed Sir Richard Plantagenet by
the King, makes a thoroughly natural jibe at his
former name, Philip, to which he had just shown such
breezy indifference. The jest could not have been
made to Lady Falconbridge without a direct insult
to her, which would have been alien to the natural,
blunt, and easygoing fondness of the relation which
Shakespeare establishes between the Bastard and his
mother. So Gurney is quite casually brought in to
receive it. But this is not enough for the Shakespeare-
drunken Coleridge.

' For an instance of Shakespeare's power *in
minimis*, I generally quote James Gurney's character
in *King John*. How individual and comical he is
with the four words allowed to his dramatic life! '

Assuredly it is not with any intention of diminishing
Coleridge's title as a Shakespearean critic that we
bring forward this instance. He is the greatest
critic of Shakespeare; and the quality of his excellence
is displayed in one of the other few notes he left on
this particular play. In Act III, scene ii., Warburton's

195

emendation of ' airy ' to ' fiery ' had in Coleridge's day been received into the text of the Bastard's lines:—

' Now by my life, this day grows wondrous hot;
Some airy devil hovers in the sky.'

On which Coleridge writes:—

' I prefer the old text: the word ' devil ' implies ' fiery.' You need only to read the line, laying a full and strong emphasis on ' devil,' to perceive the uselessness and tastelessness of Warburton's alteration.'

The test is absolutely convincing—a poet's criticism of poetry. But that Coleridge went astray not once but many times, under the influence of his idolatry of Shakespeare, corroborates the general conclusion that is forced upon any one who will take the trouble to read a whole volume of the modern *Variorum*. There has been much editing, much comment, but singularly little criticism of Shakespeare; a halfpennyworth of bread to an intolerable deal of sack. The pendulum has swung violently from niggling and insensitive textual quibble to that equally distressing exercise of human ingenuity, idealistic encomium, of which there is a typical example in the opening sentence of Mr Masefield's remarks upon the play: '' Like the best Shakespearean tragedies, *King John* is an intellectual form in which a number of people with obsessions illustrate the idea of treachery.' We remember that Mr Masefield has

196

much better than this to say of Shakespeare in his little book; but we fasten upon this sentence because it is set before us in the *Variorum*, and because it too ' is an intellectual form in which a literary man with obsessions illustrates his idea of criticism.' Genetically, it is a continuation of the shoddy element in Coleridge's Shakespeare criticism, a continual bias towards transcendental interpretation of the obvious. To take the origin a phase further back, it is the portentous offspring of the feeble constituent of German philosophy (a refusal to see the object) after it had been submitted to an idle process of ferment in the softer part of Coleridge's brain.

King John is not in the least what Mr Masefield, under this dangerous influence, has persuaded himself it is. It is simply the effort of a young man of great genius to rewrite a bad play into a good one. The effort was, on the whole, amazingly successful; that the play is only a good one, instead of a very good one, is not surprising. The miracle is that anything should have been made of *The Troublesome Raigne* at all. The *Variorum* extracts show that, of the many commentators who studied the old play with Shakespeare's version, only Swinburne saw, or had the courage to say, how utterly null the old play really is. To have made Shakespeare's Falconbridge out of the old lay figure, to have created the scenes between Hubert and John, and Hubert and Arthur, out of that decrepit skeleton—that is the work of a commanding poetical genius on the threshold of full mastery of its powers, worthy of all wonder, no doubt, but doubly worthy of close examination.

But ' ideas of treachery '! Into what cloud cuckoo

197

land have we been beguiled by Coleridge's laudanum trances ? A limbo—of this we are confident—where Shakespeare never set foot at any moment in his life, and where no robust critical intelligence can endure for a moment. We must save ourselves from this insidious disintegration by keeping our eye upon the object, and the object is just a good (not a very good) play. Not an Ibsen, a Hauptmann, a Shaw, or a Masefield play, where the influence and ravages of these ' ideas ' are certainly perceptible, but merely a Shakespeare play, one of those works of true poetic genius which can only be produced by a mind strong enough to resist every attempt at invasion by the ' idea '-bacillus.

In considering a Shakespeare play the word ' idea ' had best be kept out of the argument altogether; but there are two senses in which it might be intelligibly used. You might call the dramatic skeleton Shakespeare's idea of the play. It is the half-mechanical, half-organic factor in the work of poetic creation—the necessary means by which a poet can conveniently explicate and express his manifold æsthetic intuitions. This dramatic skeleton is governed by laws of its own, which were first and most brilliantly formulated by Aristotle in terms that, in essentials, hold good for all time. You may investigate this skeleton, seize, if you can, upon the peculiarity by which it is differentiated from all other skeletons; you may say, for instance, that *Othello* is a tragedy of jealousy, or *Hamlet* of the inhibition of self-consciousness. But if your ' idea' is to have any substance it must be moulded very closely upon the particular object with which you are dealing; and in the end you will find yourself reduced to the analysis of individual characters.

On the other hand, the word 'idea' might be intelligibly used of Shakespeare's whole attitude to the material of his contemplation, the centre of comprehension from which he worked, the aspect under which he viewed the universe of his interest. There is no reason to rest content with Coleridge's application of the epithet 'myriad-minded,' which is, at the best, an evasion of a vital question. The problem is to see Shakespeare's mind *sub specie unitatis*. It can be done; there never has been and never will be a human mind which can resist such an inquiry if it is pursued with sufficient perseverance and understanding. What chiefly stands in the way is that tradition of Shakespeariolatry which Coleridge so powerfully inaugurated, not least by the epithet 'myriad-minded.'

But of 'ideas' in any other senses than these—and in neither of these cases is 'idea' the best word for the object of search—let us beware as we would of the plague, in criticism of Shakespeare or any other great poet. Poets do not have 'ideas'; they have perceptions. They do not have an 'idea'; they have comprehension. Their creation is æsthetic, and the working of their mind proceeds from the realisation of one æsthetic perception to that of another, more comprehensive if they are to be great poets having within them the principle of poetic growth. There is undoubtedly an organic process in the evolution of a great poet, which you may, for convenience of expression, call logical; but the moment you forget that the use of the word 'logic,' in this context, is

metaphorical, you are in peril. You can follow out this
' logical process ' in a poet only by a kindred creative
process of æsthetic perception passing into æsthetic
comprehension. The hunt for ' ideas ' will only make
that process impossible; it prevents the object from
ever making its own impression upon the mind. It
has to speak with the language of logic, whereas its
use and function in the world is to speak with a
language not of logic, but of a process of mind which
is at least as sovereign in its own right as the discursive
reason.

Let us away then with ' logic ' and away with
' ideas ' from the art of literary criticism; but not, in
a foolish and impercipient reaction, to revive the
impressionistic criticism which has sapped the English
brain for a generation past. The art of criticism is
rigorous; impressions are merely its raw material;
the life-blood of its activity is in the process of
ordonnance of æsthetic impressions.

It is time, however, to return for a moment to
Shakespeare, and to observe in one crucial instance
the effect of the quest for logic in a single line. In
the fine scene where John hints to Hubert at Arthur's
murder, he speaks these lines (in the First Folio
text):—

' I had a thing to say, but let it goe:
The Sunne is in the heauen, and the proud day,
Attended with the pleasure of the world,
Is all too wanton, and too full of gawdes
To giue me audience: If the midnight bell
Did with his yron tongue, and brazen mouth
Sound on into the drowzie race of night,

If this same were a Churchyard where we stand,
And thou possessed with a thousand wrongs:
. . . Then, in despight of brooded watchfull
day,
I would into thy bosome poure my thoughts. . . .'

If one had to choose the finest line in this passage,
the choice would fall upon

' Sound on into the drowsy race of night.'

Yet you will have to look hard for it in the modern
editions of Shakespeare. At the best you will find it
with the mark of corruption:—

† ' Sound on into the drowsy race of night (' Globe ');

and you run quite a risk of finding

' Sound one into the drowsy race of night '
(' Oxford ').

There are six pages of close-printed comment upon
the line in the *Variorum*. The only reason, we can
see, why it should be the most commented line in
King John is that it is one of the most beautiful. No
one could stand it. Of all the commentators, only
one, Miss Porter, whom we name *honoris causâ*, stands
by the line with any conviction of its beauty. Every
other person either alters it or regrets his inability
to alter it.

' How can a bell sound on into a race ? ' pipe
the little editors. What is ' the race of night ? '

What *can* it mean ? How *could* a race be drowsy ?
What an *awful* contradiction in terms! And so,
while you and I, and all the other ordinary lovers of
Shakespeare are peacefully sleeping in our beds, they
come along with their little chisels, and chop out the
horribly illogical word and pop in a horribly logical
one, and we (unless we can afford the *Variorum*,
which we can't) know nothing whatever about it.
We have no redress. If we get out of our beds and
creep upon them while they are asleep—they never are
—and take out our little chisels and chop off their
horribly stupid little heads, we shall be put in prison
and Mr Justice Darling will make a horribly stupid
little joke about us. There is only one thing to do.
We must make up our minds that we have to combine
in our single person the scholar and the amateur;
we cannot trust these gentlemen.

And, indeed, they have been up to their little
games elsewhere in *King John*. They do not like
the reply of the citizens of Angiers to the summons
of the rival kings:—

> ' A greater powre than We denies all this,
> And till it be undoubted, we do locke
> Our former scruple in our strong-barr'd gates;
> Kings of our feare, untill our feares resolu'd
> Be by some certaine king, purg'd and depos'd.'

Admirable sense, excellent poetry. But no! We
must not have it. Instead we are given ' King'd
of our fears ' (' Globe ') or ' Kings of ourselves '
(' Oxford '). Bad sense, bad poetry.

They do not like Pandulph's speech to France:—

' France, thou maist hold a serpent by the tongue,
A cased lion by the mortall paw,
A fasting tiger safer by the tooth
Than keep in peace that hand which thou dost
hold.'

' Cased,' caged, is too much for them. We must
have ' chafed,' in spite of

' If thou would'st not entomb thyself alive
And case thy reputation in thy tent.'

Again, the Folio text of the meeting between the
Bastard and Hubert in Act V., when Hubert fails to
recognise the Bastard's voice, runs thus:—

' Unkinde remembrance: thou and endles night,
Have done me shame: Brave Soldier, pardon
me
That any accent breaking from thy tongue
Should scape the true acquaintaince of mine
eare.'

This time ' endless ' is not poetical enough for the
editors. Theobald's emendation ' eyeless ' is received
into the text. One has only to read the brief scene
through to realise that Hubert is wearied and obsessed
by the night that will never end. He is overwrought
by his knowledge of

' news fitting to the night,
Black, fearful, comfortless, and horrible,'

and by his long wandering in search of the Bastard:—

> ' Why, here I walk in the black brow of night
> To find you out.'

Yet the dramatically perfect ' endless ' has had
to make way for the dramatically stupid ' eyeless.'
Is it surprising that we do not trust these gentlemen ?

[APRIL, 1920